JI

J

M

The Art of Helping People Effectively

The Art of Helping

People Effectively

STANLEY C. MAHONEY

ASSOCIATION PRESS ■ NEW YORK

Publisher's stock number: 1644

Library of Congress catalog card number: 67-14588

Printed in the United States of America

By this term (helping relationship) I mean a relationship in which at least one of the parties has the intent of promoting the growth, development, maturity, improved functioning, improved coping with life of the other. The other, in this sense, may be one individual or a group. To put it in another way, a helping relationship might be defined as one in which one of the participants intends that there should come about, in one or both parties, more appreciation of, more expression of, more functional use of the latent inner resources of the individual.

. . . if I can form a helping relationship to myself—if I can be sensitively aware of and acceptant toward my own feelings—then the likelihood is great that I can form a helping relationship toward another.

. . . the optimal helping relationship is the kind of relationship created by a person who is psychologically mature. Or to put it in another way, the degree to which I can create relationships which facilitate the growth of others as separate persons is a measure of the growth I have achieved in myself. In some respects this is a disturbing thought, but it is also a promising or challenging one. It would indicate that if I am interested in creating helping relationships I have a fascinating life-time job ahead of me, stretching and developing my potentialities in the direction of growth.

—CARL R. ROGERS
"The Characteristics of a Helping Relationship," *Personnel and Guidance Journal,* 1958, 37, 6-16

Foreword

The Art of Helping People Effectively is both a symptom of, and an aid to, a basic reorientation that is occurring in our American value system during the latter half of the twentieth century. The early days of our republic were marked by unabashed humanism, which gave rise to a system of government without parallel in the history of mankind for its subtle and effective blend of idealism and practicality. Territorial expansion, waves of immigrants from diverse cultures, recurrent depressions, the War Between the States, and two major world conflicts considerably disrupted and impaired the orderly development of American culture. Humanism gave way to materialism, idealism to opportunism, and an egalitarianism to class consciousness.

But now we are witnessing a reawakening and rebirth of the American conscience and of our uniquely American vision of society. The War on Poverty, the civil rights movement, long-overdue attention to equality of educational opportunity, revisions in sexual morality, innovations in traditional religious thinking—and this book—are all symptomatic of our national determination to complete the American Revolution. The basic conviction that lies behind all of these movements is that the individual is his own reason for existing, and that the day-by-day existence of all of us as human beings must have inherent meaning and dignity. No longer can the mean and squalid here-and-now reality be pushed aside by alibis about the immutability of human society, nor dispelled by guarantees of future rewards.

It is in this spirit that this book is written. It offers an extremely useful tool to all of us who are involved in attempting to improve the quality of human existence in our time. It is a reaffirmation of our conviction that human beings can and must be of help to each other, and that it is only through such interdependency and mutual assistance that society can serve the needs of its individual members. Dr. Mahoney has brought to this book a sophisticated and mature understanding of the key contributions of the several behavioral sciences, and has translated them into pragmatic and workable suggestions for professional and nonprofessional, full and part-time helper alike. Whether the reader is a neighborhood aide in the War on Poverty, a psychiatric technician in a hospital or clinic, a volunteer working in a health or social agency, a case aide beginning service in a welfare department, or a school or college counselor, he will find this book of inestimable assistance in increasing his effectiveness in helping others.

H. G. Whittington, M.D.
Director of Psychiatric Services
Denver Department of Health
    and Hospitals
Denver, Colorado

Acknowledgements

To acknowledge by name the help of all of those who have contributed to the development of the thoughts expressed in this book would be a virtual impossibility. Yet it would be a gross oversight not to acknowledge at least in a general way the help received from countless numbers of individuals over the years. It is truly a humbling and deeply satisfying experience to attempt to integrate and to put on paper one's thoughts about effective helping; with each page memories of experiences in giving and receiving help that had long since faded became vivid again.

Certainly family experiences assume a prominent position in the parade of memories. It is with deep love and respect that I dedicate this book to the memory of my father, to my mother, to my wife, and to my three children. To my wife, Martha, and to my children Linda, David, and Kathleen go my special thanks for helping me live with myself and with them in some semblance of a helpful husband and father while writing this book. In particular, the thought-provoking comments of my wife with regard to the developing manuscript were invaluable and in keeping with a true spirit of helping.

With nearly every page other memories were evoked of former teachers, supervisors, colleagues, students, clients and patients. The stimulation received from these individuals and the insights gained from relationships with them were major influences in shaping the thoughts expressed in the following pages. To Dr. David Proctor, Dr. H. G. Whittington, Mr. G. C. Coniglio, Miss Susan

Ellermeier, Mr. Timothy Schumacher, Miss Marcial Burroughs, and Mrs. Vivian Umbarger go my sincere thanks and appreciation for their helpful comments on all or part of the manuscript.

To the extent that this book is helpful, credit is due in no small part to them; to the extent that it falls short, I alone must take responsibility.

To avoid possible confusion and misinterpretation with respect to the contents of this book, and since I am currently employed as Consultant in Clinical Psychology in the Denver Regional Office of the National Institute of Mental Health, it is important to state that the views and opinions expressed in this book are solely my own and are not to be construed as official opinions or views of the National Institute of Mental Health, United States Public Health Service, or Department of Health, Education and Welfare.

STANLEY C. MAHONEY, PH.D.

Westminster, Colorado

Contents

Introduction

The consideration of three facts and three assumptions have resulted in the preparation of this book. The first fact is that we all at times have feelings and emotions which we experience as unpleasant and painful. We encounter difficulties from time to time both in living with ourselves and in living with others. We have what are commonly called "personal problems," although they usually involve others as well as ourselves and are frequently problems only insofar as we feel inadequate to cope with them or are unable to accept them. We experience discomfort from thoughts and feelings that arise from within ourselves, and we experience discomfort from actions and events that occur outside ourselves. We experience difficulty in communicating to others and making ourselves understood, and we experience difficulty in understanding what others are trying to comunicate to us. We suffer from difficulties of our own making, and we suffer from the inevitabilities of life over which we have no control. Confronted with physical illness, separation from a loved one, educational and vocational decisions, seeking a mate, the unfamiliarity of a new job, the birth of a baby, retirement, and many other aspects of life, we frequently experience feelings of insecurity, inadequacy, loneliness, indecision, doubt, fear, and anxiety. We are all human and there is no immunity for human suffering—we all hurt at times.

The second fact is that we all seek help for our personal problems. We seek help with varying degrees of awareness about what we are doing, but there are times when we all need and use others in resolving our emotional difficulties. The person who never needs help and who never seeks help is as mythical as the self-made man; complete self-sufficiency is an illusion of our own making. We seek help not only in a variety of ways, some verbal and some nonverbal, but from a variety of sources ranging from family, relatives, and friends to social workers, psychologists, and psychiatrists.

The third fact is that we all give help to others who are experiencing emotional difficulties. There is probably no one who has not been approached by another, directly or indirectly, seeking help for a personal problem. We have all felt at times the anguish of wanting to help but not knowing how; we have also experienced the satisfying feeling of having helped in some way. We have all overshot the mark, helping too much, too soon, too fast; we have all undershot the mark, helping too little, too late, and too slow. Emotional disturbances and personal problems are not all of equal severity. While some require professional help, others can be resolved through the help of family and friends. The necessity for professional help frequently arises as a consequence of inadequate helping relationships that have existed in the home, the school, and the community. The effectiveness of professional help is always dependent, in part, upon the extent to which the individual receives appropriate help from family and friends. Mental health, the emotional well-being of ourselves and others, is the concern and responsibility of all of us. Aware of it or not, we are involved.

The first assumption is that there are similarities among all helping relationships, regardless of the special problems involved. There is always someone seeking help, someone giving help, and a relationship between these individuals. There are attitudes and feelings on the part of both individuals involved about giving help and receiving help which influence the effectiveness of the helping process. There are communication aspects to all helping relationships. There are also social and cultural values and practices which serve to define the helping relationship and how it will be anticipated and experienced by both individuals involved.

The second assumption is that we can learn to become more effective in the art of helping others regardless of the level of our effectiveness at the present time. Helping others, like all behavioral patterns and endeavors, develops through learning and practice. As with other skills, we vary individually with respect to our potentialities and limitations for being effective helpers; but this should not discourage us from developing our capacities in this endeavor to the utmost.

The third assumption is that the first step toward becoming more effective in the art of helping is to increase our awareness of the complexities involved in the process. Success in the art of helping depends upon our understanding of ourselves and others in the context of what we are trying to accomplish. Although awareness and understanding alone are not sufficient to make us effective helpers, without them our effectiveness can be greatly impaired.

The purpose of this book is both to inform and to stimulate. It is hoped that the information that is presented about the art of helping will stimulate you to reflect and to ponder, by yourself and with others, on your own significance and insignificance in the art of helping so that you may be better able to be of genuine help to your fellow man. If you do not find yourself with questions about helping that you did not have before reading these pages, if you do not experience some degree of confusion about what it means to help another help himself, then this book has not achieved its purpose. And if your aroused feelings and thoughts do not lead you to take the second step for becoming a more effective helper, that of verbalizing your reactions with others, then this book has also fallen short of its purpose. As with all helping relationships, the success of the process depends on all involved; this book will meet with its greatest successes in the hands of those who use it only as a starting place.

This book was written for individuals who find themselves vocationally in strategic positions for helping others with emotional and behavioral difficulties even though their primary responsibilities might be with other endeavors: for teachers, pastors, policemen, nurses, supervisors, and many others. It was written for the many individuals who volunteer their services during leisure hours to help others: for Scout Leaders and Little League coaches, for Gray Ladies and Den Mothers, for volunteers in mental hospitals and in prisons, and for many others. It was written for the dormitory counselor, the Big Brother, and the camp leader; for the parent who would help his child and the youth who would help his parent; for the student who is planning to enter a helping profession.

This book was written as a second-best measure—second-best

because we would find it far more beneficial if we could explore, discuss, and share together our thoughts about what it means to help others help themselves. If we could sit on the proverbial log together and talk, we could accomplish far more. Since this is not possible, I have attempted to put my thoughts on paper in much the same way that I might say them to you if we were together. Thus you will find the style of this book more informal than formal, with rigid organization being sacrificed at times to allow the expression of thoughts that come to mind which, strictly considered, would be somewhat irrelevant. You will find also that the same thought or idea will frequently occur in different contexts, and be examined from different perspectives, just as it would if we were talking together.

This is not a how-to-do-it-yourself book with one-two-three steps. Human relationships seldom permit such rigidity. But it might be called a "be-it-yourself" book in that it emphasizes an attitude of "being-for-others" and "being-with-others" rather than "doing-for-others." It is not a book that will make you an "expert" in helping others, although hopefully it will make you more aware of both your capacities and limitations for helping others.

Considerable use is made of examples in an effort to make the material as meaningful as possible. The examples used are typical and representative, not descriptive of specific situations that have occurred or people that I have known. Any similarities to specific people living or dead is purely coincidental.

This book will be helpful to the extent that you are ready to take an active part in a helping process. Read actively, not passively, and let your own thoughts interact with the material on the printed page. Reflect on your own experiences that come to mind as you read, for by so doing the material presented will take on greater meaning and depth. Share your thoughts concerning what you read with others. As you discuss it and argue about it, you will be increasing your understanding of what it means to help another help himself. Ultimately you will increase your effectiveness in the art of helping.

1

Helping Others: Orientation and Goals

▶Helping others to help themselves is an attitude of wanting to use ourselves in a manner that will be most beneficial to the well-being of another. It is a belief that we can act altruistically and place the interests of another before our own. It is a belief that one of the greatest satisfactions an individual can experience is the process of developing and actualizing his own capacities to be and to do. It is a faith that we can help ourselves and others, a faith in people. It is positive thinking on a very broad and deep basis about man's capacity to help himself, and to obtain perspective on both his significance and insignificance in the helping process. Helping others is a necessity for human survival.

When we say that we want to help someone we are saying that we want to have an effect in his life or on whatever he is doing. We want our being there to make a difference. Let us face directly that the effect of our being there, the effect of our attempt to help, can have either positive or negative results. Whether we would call the result positive or negative depends upon our values and the expectations that we bring to the helping relationship. We also have to recognize that others might view our effect differently; they might call positive that which we would call negative, or negative that which we would call positive.

WHEN TO HELP?

Mrs. Jones looks out her window and sees her son David fighting with another boy his age in the backyard. They are really having at it, and the match looks rather even. Mrs. Jones is not sure whether to let them continue or to stop the fight. As she stands at the window in doubt, her boy David goes down with the other boy on top of him. Mrs. Jones now decides; enough is enough, and she now must step in to help. She rushes out and stops the fight. She feels relieved for a moment, thinking that she has prevented David from becoming seriously hurt. She would probably feel at this moment that she has helped in a positive manner. But what about David? More than likely he is now venting his anger at mother for having, as he phrases it, "interfered." As he goes grudgingly into the house he gripes, "Oh, ma, what'd you have to do that for. I could have whipped him." As David sees it, his mother has not helped him and the effect of her having been there is essentially negative. She views her "helping" as positive, thinking of the beating she has saved him; he views her "helping" as negative, thinking of what the gang will say.

How do we know when we are really helping? How can we be sure we are not harming? Is our influence more positive or more negative? These are questions we can frequently never answer definitively, for there are usually many answers, not just one. Different individuals, with different values and goals in mind, will evaluate differently the effects of any attempt to help.

Who is to say who is right? Who is to say whether a given action will be helpful or not? Humbly and with full recognition that the individual you are attempting to help may see it differently and that you can be wrong, you are going to have to come to a decision as to whether your action or presence would be helpful or not. You really don't have any choice many times. Mrs. Jones could not evade this question. Once she saw David and the other boy fighting, she had to make a decision as to how best she could help David. There were several courses of action open to her: she could have left them completely alone, she could have let the fight continue and served as a referee, she could have stopped the fight and arranged for the boys to put on boxing gloves in the school gym, or she could have stopped the fight. Like Mrs. Jones, we frequently find that we have choices, but that we do not always have a choice over our choices. If we are motivated to help another, we have to decide what would be most helpful.

GUIDELINES TO HELPING ANOTHER

When we are actively engaged in trying to be of help, we frequently become bogged down in immediate details and lose sight of long-range consequences. Under the pressures of the moment we forget what is important. The following six questions are presented as guidelines for determining whether we are really helping another to help himself. The long-range goal is to help others function in a mature and responsible manner, making productive use of their capacities and finding satisfaction in life while not interfering with others doing the same. The six questions are concerned with six fundamental characteristics generally found in mature and responsible individuals. The six characteristics are not presented in order of importance; all can be considered equally important. Although at times our primary concern may be with just one or two of them, we must never wholly lose sight of the others if we are to be really helpful. To become overconcerned with just one, to the exclusion of the others, is to be like one of the blind men trying to find out what an elephant looks like. As you may remember, the blind men touched different parts of the elephant and came to different conclusions, all equally distorted, about what the elephant looked like.

1. *Will I be helping the person to become more realistic?* Being realistic means attempting to understand the nature of ourselves, others, and the world around us and functioning in a manner consistent with our knowledge. It means being aware of the consequences that follow certain actions, whether the actions be those of people or objects. It means being aware of the complexities of cause-and-effect relationships, and differentiating between these and coincidental relationships. It means becoming aware of and accepting what "is" before making decisions about what "should be." It means bringing aspirations into reasonable harmony with capacities and limitations.

The Greek challenge "know thyself" and the Shakespearian command "this above all, to thine own self be true" are reflected in the realistic person's effort to understand himself. He accepts the reality of his physical and psychological functioning, and recognizes that he has a wide variety of needs, feelings, and thoughts. He strives to become aware of and to accept both his similarities to and differences from other people. He accepts the world of social reality that he is born into just as he accepts the world of physical reality; this does not mean that he will never seek to change it, but rather that he will attempt to understand it as it exists before he makes a decision as to whether it ought to be changed.

The person who is realistic attempts to base his decisions and actions upon reason and intellect rather than impulse and emotion. He accepts that he will frequently have to forego immediate pleasure if he is to achieve long-range goals. Dreams and fantasies have a place in his life, but he attempts to differentiate between these and facts. He does not deny the values of romanticism and idealism, recognizing that his striving to be realistic is an ideal. He accepts change and uncertainty as part of life, and some anxiety and suffering as inevitable consequences of being human. He accepts both his need for meaningful relationships with other individuals and his need to be alone.

The realistic individual is a seeker of knowledge and truth, and he displays a curiosity toward all things. He values honest thinking more than positive thinking, and he abhors ignorance and hypocrisy above all else. He is realistic enough to accept that he will not be realistic at all times, that he will need freedom from the demands of being realistic. Hence he is realistic enough to let himself be unrealistic at the appropriate time and place.

2. *Will I be helping the person to feel more self-confident and adequate?* Feeling self-confident and personally adequate means having faith in our capacities to do what has to be done and to be accepting of that which can only be accepted. It means feeling "I can" more than "I can't," and "I am" more than "I am not." It means feeling "I've got what it takes" more than "I don't have what it takes." It is feeling "I am good" and "I am important." This quality is reflected in a basically optimistic approach to life and a looking forward to tomorrow and the future with hope more than fear.

Feeling self-confident is not a New Year's resolution kind of "I will" or a "whistling in the dark." It does not develop from positive thinking that is primarily an attempt to deny the realities of life. It develops from honest evaluation and acceptance of ourselves, others, and the world around us. It develops from experiences in living, and from having failed as well as having succeeded.

It develops from having stayed around to find out that "the roof won't fall in" when the pressure and anxiety have been high. It develops from warm relationships with other people who trust us and have faith in us—from having made mistakes, from having been embarrassed, and from having made fools of ourselves. It comes from having developed intellectual, emotional, social, and physical competencies which enable us to cope successfully with problems, frustrations, and crises. It is seeking the challenge of tomorrow rather than fearing the frustration of tomorrow.

3. *Will I be helping the person to become more self-directing?* Self-direction means assuming responsibility for one's own life. It means moving from the total dependence of infancy, which carries no responsibilities, to the relative independence of maturity with its consequent responsibilities. It means facing the question, "What do I want to do with my life?" It means facing the question, "What kind of a person do I want to be?"

Being self-directing means making decisions and attempting to solve problems, rather than passively avoiding decision and action because of the risk of mistake and failure. It means taking the consequences for our actions rather than trying to justify them on the basis of what father, mother, wife or husband did or did not do or say. It means becoming free from the tyranny of our own impulses as well as the tyranny of what others have in mind for us. It means developing sound values that enable us to control our impulses appropriately, not deny them. It requires self-awareness as to what we are doing and why we are doing it, not blind automatic functioning. It requires that we respond with awareness rather than react with impulse.

Being self-directing means striving to become the kind of person we want to become, which may or may not be different from the kind of person someone else wants us to become. It does not mean being nonconformist for the sake of being different or being conformist because we dare not to be otherwise. It means accepting the fact that others will give us advice, and also accepting the fact that we need not always act on the basis of it. It means being able to say "No" as well as "Yes" to the requests others make of us. It means recognizing that, in the last analysis, we cannot escape the fact of having to live with ourselves.

4. *Will I be helping the person to become more self-actualizing?* The self-actualizing person seeks to develop and use his capacities and potentialities to the fullest. Life, for him, is a continuous

process of becoming and doing rather than a state of having achieved. The self-actualizing person's behavior is characterized by curiosity, spontaneity, and creativity. The unknown and the uncertain are not avoided or merely tolerated; they are looked upon as providing the zest to life.

For the self-actualizing person the maintenance of life through the satisfaction of basic physical and psychological needs is not enough; rather maintenance of life is a necessity that must be attended to so that growth and development can proceed. Work and play are not sharply differentiated; both are viewed as ways of actualizing potentialities. The self-actualizing person's interests and concerns are broad and varied; his greatest frustration is not "what shall I do or be," but rather, "how will I ever do all that I want to do and be all that I want to be." Self-actualizing people are individuals who tend to jump gladly into the stream of life, waiting neither to be pushed by internal pressures nor to be pulled by external forces.

5. *Will I be helping the person to rejoice in being alive?* The person who rejoices in being alive is enthusiastic about life and values the preciousness of the moment "here and now." He not only accepts; he enjoys. He experiences pleasure from his sensations and he finds beauty in the world around him—the warmth of the sun, the sharpness of the wind, the clouds in the sky are experienced freshly and keenly. Realistic understanding increases his capacity to enjoy anew and afresh, and he retains the childhood capacity to find delight and wonder in the experience of the moment. A rainbow is experienced as wonderful and beautiful, not merely understood as a phenomenon of physics. The warm glow of a campfire is felt as an experience, not just understood as a chemical reaction.

To the person who rejoices in being alive, life is never dull, but always exciting whether it be painful or pleasurable. It is not the positive thinking born out of desperation that "life can be beautiful"; it is the deeply felt "life is beautiful." It is the counterpart of knowing in breadth and in depth, and it develops from feeling deeply and widely. It is to understand emotionally as well as intellectually. It is to feel life deeply satisfying with all its joys and sorrows as well as with its triumphs and tribulations.

6. *Will I be helping the individual to become more considerate of others?* The individual who is considerate of others does not achieve his own ends at their expense. On the contrary, he tends to

achieve his own ends in compatible harmony with others doing the same. His basic attitudes toward others are ones of helping rather than exploiting, trusting rather than suspecting, and loving rather than hating. He tends to be aware of the needs and strivings of others as well as his own. He seeks individuals who can work and live in harmony with him rather than trying to change others to become like himself. He respects and recognizes differences without always having to evaluate in terms of "better than" or "worse than" me. He achieves success in his own eyes and in the eyes of the world through his own being and doing rather than through criticizing and belittling the efforts of others.

The person who is considerate of others respects the rights of others to be self-directing and self-actualizing, and he seeks to foster their efforts in this direction as much by not intervening as by intervening in their lives. He does not build his own self-confidence at the expense of others. He joins with others in rejoicing in life. But he does not tolerate major acts of inconsiderateness of others toward him. As he is considerate of them, he expects and demands the same in return. To do otherwise would be to make a mockery of considerateness toward others.

These six characteristics—being realistic, self-confident, self-directing, self-actualizing, considerate of others, and rejoicing in life—are, to a greater or lesser degree, goals to be kept in mind whenever we want to help another help himself. These are the long-range, important goals. Usually, although not always, they tend to blend together and the attaining of one of them fosters the attaining of the others. In Biblical terms, it is truly a case of "for whosoever hath, to him shall be given . . . but whosoever hath not, from him shall be taken away even that he hath."

We never learn just one thing at a time. We are always learning many things on many different levels at the same time. When we are striving for a very specific goal, or seeking to solve a very specific problem, or attempting to cope with our feelings of anxiety in a crisis, we are also learning about becoming realistic and self-confident and self-directing.

A CASE ILLUSTRATION

Let us take a specific example. Mr. Johnson is a coach for the Little League team and at the moment he wants to help Johnny become a better batter. The immediate, specific goal is to help

Johnny increase his batting average. By respecting Johnny's decision as to whether he wants to increase his batting average or not, or even whether he wants to play ball or not, Mr. Johnson will be fostering Johnny's capacity for self-direction. Mr. Johnson will have to display some realistic functioning on his own part in deciding whether the immediate goal or the long-range goal is most important. If he is interested primarily in helping Johnny to help himself, then in this situation he will probably recognize that there are many other goals Johnny can pursue which are as important as increasing his batting average. And he will probably respect Johnny's capacity to choose his own goal.

Johnny is interested in increasing his batting average, however, so Mr. Johnson lets him know that he will be glad to help him and give him some pointers. Again being realistic, he does not frighten Johnny away by pushing his help upon him; rather, he lets Johnny know he is willing to help and then has faith in Johnny's self-directing capacities to let Johnny decide whether he wants to make use of the available help or not. He is realistic enough to know that he can extend the helping hand but that the other fellow has to grasp it if it is really to help. Johnny feels a little anxious and embarrassed; after all, this is the coach and he doesn't want the coach to think he doesn't know how to bat. Also, he knows he gets scared when he gets up to the plate and the ball is thrown at him—it sure looks that way when he is standing there—and he sure doesn't want the coach to find out that he's afraid. But he does want to bat better and the coach does know how it's done. Johnny's self-actualizing tendencies lead him to accept the help.

The coach is not so blinded by his own need for a good team or by his own love of the game that he does not recognize some of Johnny's conflicts. Being realistic, he knows that some boys are afraid and helps Johnny to accept the reality of his own fear by not trying to deny it or belittle it or talk it away. He does not shame Johnny for having honest feelings. Instead, he shows Johnny how he can cope with his fear by becoming more aware of some of the realities of batting a ball. Both by word and by example he shows Johnny how to grasp the bat, stand at the plate, and so on. Johnny feels his self-confidence growing as he begins to catch on. The self-confidence and calmness of the coach are reassuring, and the words of praise—meaningful because they are honest and not lavish—for his efforts send a further glow through him. As he becomes more competent, he feels less afraid; as he feels more self-confident, he begins to rejoice in the experience of the moment. The better he feels, the better he does, and the more he wants to do.

Learning to bat a ball could have been many things to Johnny. It could have been a humiliating, agonizing experience in which he felt rejected, defeated, hurt, and misunderstood. It could have left him feeling hostile toward authority figures and sure that they would be against him. It could have fostered an attitude of "what's the sense of trying, you can't win anyway." But Johnny was fortunate. For him it was very much a growth experience that had positive effects far beyond batting a ball. What about considerateness toward others? If this experience had done nothing to foster that, it would have still been a good example of helping others to help themselves. As it was, Johnny received perhaps the greatest lesson in being considerate toward others that one can receive—he had been shown by Mr. Johnson's behavior what being considerate means. He had not been told a lesson; he had experienced a lesson in considerateness.

THE OPTION OF HELPING

Helping others to help themselves can be a large part of our lives or a small part of our lives. For some, an attitude of helping others will be a general approach to almost all their relationships with other people. For others, an attitude of helping others will be dominant in only a few of their relationships with people. Many of the roles necessary in modern civilization require that we relate to others in ways which cannot be considered dominated by a helping motive. Basically selling is not dominated by the helping motive—the primary goal is to sell the product. It is a technique of selling, unfortunately quite successful, to convince others that you are there to help them rather than to sell them. Sometimes we even convince ourselves that we want to sell something to someone only to help them. Let us at least be honest and call a spade a spade. There are many roles in our society that require attitudes other than a helping one, and this does not make them or us necessarily bad or wrong. The basically dishonest act is the extent to which we fool ourselves or others as to our true motives and intents in an attempt to use another's need for help to our own advantage.

The burden of feeling that we always have to function in a way that is helpful to others is as unrealistic as the view that we can avoid our helping responsibilities altogether. The truth, as is usual, is to be found at neither extreme. We have helping responsibilities which we cannot avoid without being harmful to the growth and development of another, and we have helping opportunities that we can choose not to exercise without being actively harmful to another. There is a difference between being non-helpful and actively harmful.

In many of our daily activities we are being neither helpful nor harmful to others, but rather just non-helpful. Some of these activities are entered into out of necessity, such as sleeping and eating. Other activities are entered into out of choice, such as knitting and reading, and may be done alone. To feel we must always be helping others directly, and to feel unworthy or sinful when we are not, is being unrealistic and actually impairing our capacity to help at other times. We not only have to meet our own needs, both physical and psychological, but we also can choose to use our time in ways that are non-helpful without being harmful to others.

There are some roles in our lives, however, which require us to be directly intent upon helping another help himself. Thus, as husband or wife, father or mother, we have helping responsibilities that we cannot avoid without harming another. When we assumed these roles, we assumed helping responsibilities whether we were aware of them or not. We must not only decide how large a part helping others to help themselves is going to play in our lives, but also we must decide whom we are going to help and be aware that there are some who need our help more than others.

In my work with children I have heard more than one son ask about his father, "But why can't he help me like he helps the other guys?" Junior is not aware of all the complexities of life, including the helping behavior of his father. In his naiveness he frequently asks the telling question. He knows that it hurts when father has time to give to the other fellows but not to himself. He is humanly and honestly selfish: he wants father to himself. Not all the time, but some of the time. He wants a chance to impress father, to please father, to love father; to be important, respected, and loved by father. He wants to have his time in the sun with one of the most important people in his life. Many a father-son relationship has floundered badly while father was giving himself to others.

Because of your role as a mother or father, wife or husband, son or daughter, you are able to give a kind of help to your loved ones that no one else can give. You are important to them just because you are you. If you really want to help others, then you cannot avoid the question as to who needs your help most. Are you avoiding helping where you could help most in order to help where you can help easiest? Are your helping activities serving the double purpose of providing an escape from helping responsibilities at home and a means of easing your guilts for this escape?

To the son or daughter who yearns to be closer to his parents, it makes little difference whether the parents are Scout leaders, Brownie leaders, out hunting, or playing bridge. To the wife struggling with her own loneliness and her need for male companionship, it makes little difference whether husband is playing poker or helping the youth group at the church. It is not enough merely to be able to say, "but I was helping others"; this does not always help the person that only you could help.

Because helping others is not just a simple matter of giving way to our impulses, we must also recognize that there are times when others can help our loved ones more effectively than we can. If we become too emotionally involved with trying to help someone else, then our own needs and wishes tend to dominate our behavior and we lose perspective on what might be best for the other person. We start with good intentions, but our anxieties may result in our hurting more than helping. Thus, the mother who attempts to help her child with his homework may find that her "helping" has become irritable pushing or has resulted in her doing all the homework herself. When this kind of situation develops, the better part of helping may be to let somone else do the helping.

Helping others to help themselves is not always easy, and it is seldom simple. Like many other things that we do it requires motivation, understanding, and effort from us if we want to do it effectively. It requires not only our intention to use ourselves in a way that will be beneficial to another, but also our willingness to engage in some hard, honest thinking and wondering about ourselves and others. How effective we will be in helping others to help themselves will depend largely upon how successful we are in becoming realistic, self-confident, self-directing, self-actualizing, considerate of others, and rejoiceful of life ourselves. Our example will usually speak louder than our words.

2

Human Behavior

▶If we are going to be effective in helping others to help themselves, then we must base our attempts to help on realistic understanding rather than on misconceptions and wishful thinking. Our helping behavior must be based on honest thinking as much as positive thinking if it is to be really helpful. The information presented in this chapter is fundamental and descriptive of normal, average people and everyday human functioning; it is not about abnormal and deviant behavior.

A great variety of examples could be used to illustrate the material in this chapter. Since we are interested in increasing our effectiveness in helping others, most examples will involve some aspect of helping behavior. As we learn about human behavior, we will also learn something about helping others. We will be learning not only about the functioning of individuals we might want to help, but also about ourselves. Effectiveness in helping others depends as much upon our awareness and understanding of ourselves as it does upon our awareness and understanding of others.

GENERAL CHARACTERISTICS

We will start with four general characteristics of all human behavior. First, human behavior is complex and any specific behavioral pattern has many causes, not just one. This is sometimes called the principle of multiple causation. We never do anything for just one simple reason; there are always several reasons or factors or causes as to why we behave as we do. Many times one or two factors may be most important or dominant in determining why we behave as we do, but this does not mean that there are no other factors influencing our behavior at the time. Whenever we want to understand the behavior of ourselves or someone else, we must never look for just one cause or reason; we must always attempt to become aware of the many possible factors that are involved. Whenever we glibly explain someone's behavior as being due to one reason, one factor, or one cause, then we are committing a very common and very serious error—the error of oversimplification.

Second, human behavior is caused by factors that may be conscious or unconscious or both. That is, our behavior is determined by factors which we may or may not be aware of. Much as we would like to think of ourselves as rational and logical beings, we have to recognize that we are never as rational and logical as we think we are. Our thinking and our deciding do not take place in a vacuum; they are influenced by our feelings and needs, by our wishes and hopes, and by our fears and anxieties. Just because we are not consciously aware of our needs, wishes, and fears does not mean that they are not influencing our behavior. In our efforts to be as realistic and as aware as possible, we must also recognize that we will seldom, if ever, be aware of all the factors determining any specific behavioral pattern. We can, however, strive to be as aware as possible of the major factors involved and accept the human limitation of probably not being aware of all factors.

Third, human behavior is influenced by factors both inside and outside the individual. Inner determinants of behavior may include physical factors, such as lack of sleep or the effect of alcohol; emotional factors, such as the desire to be liked or the effects of anxiety; and intellectual factors, such as our ability to think logically or our capacity to memorize. Outer determinants of behavior include physical factors, such as the weather or the distance to a certain place; social factors, such as the reactions of others and the demands of being a member of a certain group; and cultural factors, such as traditions that have been operating for a long time. Sometimes inner factors will be dominant in determining behavior and sometimes outer factors will be dominant. Usually both inner and outer factors will be influencing our behavior.

Fourth, human behavior is influenced by past experience. Our behavior is not just the result of the interaction of inner and outer factors; it is also the result of how we interpret and react to these inner and outer factors. And this interpretation and reaction will be influenced to a large degree by our past experiences. We will tend to respond in ways that worked for us in the past and that resulted in pleasure and success; we will tend to avoid responding in ways that brought us pain and failure in the past. Sometimes our previous ways of responding will be effective for us again, and sometimes they will not be effective because the situation has changed or we have changed. Present behavior reflects, to a large extent, what has been learned in the past. An individual's present behavior is usually much more understandable when viewed in the context of his previous experiences.

Human behavior is complex, and if we are going to be effective in helping others to help themselves, we must first accept this complexity. To the extent that we attempt to take the easy way out and oversimplify either our own or someone else's behavior we will be impairing our capacity to help. In fact, it is the human tendency to oversimplify that many times is an important factor in aggravating our problems and difficulties. We frequently feel safer and more secure when we think we know the reason for something, and we feel more anxious and uncomfortable when we do not feel we know the reason. In our effort to avoid anxiety in the face of uncertainty and to feel secure, we frequently oversimplify and obtain only a temporary security that later proves harmful to ourselves and others. The more we can accept the human limitation of not knowing all the reasons and causes for a person's behavior, the more helpful we will probably be to the person.

A CASE ILLUSTRATION

Let us now examine these four general characteristics of human behavior in the context of a concrete example. Mrs. Martin has volunteered to be a Gray Lady and help in her local hospital. If asked why she volunteered her time and services, she would probably reply that she wants to do something for other people and now that her children are in school she has sufficient time to be able to give a few hours a week to the Gray Ladies. Her husband might say that her stay in the hospital a few months ago has something to do with it and that she just likes being a part of hospital life. Her children might tell you she is doing it because she always has to be doing something and if she isn't in one group she is in another. A neighbor might mention the fact that many of her friends are Gray Ladies and that she volunteered primarily because her friends were doing it. Another neighbor might say that she is doing it just so she can dress up and go out and get away from home. Another acquaintance might say she is doing it because her husband thinks it is "good for business" if she is active in community affairs. In actuality, Mrs. Martin's helping behavior might reflect all of these factors and many others also. She is probably aware of some of the factors influencing her behavior, but not all of them. Her past experiences as well as factors in the present situation, both inside and outside herself, have influenced her decision to become a Gray Lady.

How effective Mrs. Martin will be as a Gray Lady will not depend upon the fact that there is more than one reason for her wanting to be one. If she is not aware of this, however, and if she reacts as if she were insulted when someone mentions a reason for her behavior other than purely wanting to help someone else, then her helping effectiveness will probably be impaired. She will be better able to help the patients in the hospital when she is comfortable with the fact that she, also, is obtaining satisfaction from her helping activity and in a variety of ways. What is most important is her awareness and acceptance of the major factors influencing her decision to help others as a Gray Lady so that she will be able to control her behavior appropriately. To the extent that we tend to be unrealistic and deny the reasons for our behavior, then we will be less able to act in a way that we want to act.

MEETING BASIC NEEDS

As human beings we all have basic physical and psychological needs which must be satisfied to some degree if we are to function in a comfortable and effective manner. When our basic needs are not fulfilled to some degree, then these needs will tend to dominate our thinking, decision-making, and actions. Basic physical and psychological needs have sometimes been called maintenance needs because they must be satisfied at least to a minimal degree before we are able to rationally and consciously decide what kind of a person we want to be and what we want to do with our lives.

The achievement of some measure of stability in meeting our basic needs is a prerequisite for effective functioning in helping others to help themselves.

If a rose bush is to produce roses effectively, then certain conditions necessary to the maintenance of the rose bush must first be met. If these conditions are not met, then the bush will tend to use its energies and resources to maintain itself rather than to produce beautiful roses. A rose grower first makes sure that the bush itself is adequately maintained before he strives to enable it to produce roses. Just like the rose bush, we first have to attend to our own basic maintenance needs if we want to be effective in carrying out our intentions and purposes in life. If one of our intentions is to help others, then we must first make sure that our own maintenance needs are not going to interfere unduly with our carrying out this purpose.

On a physical level we have, among others, needs for food, water, sleep, oxygen, and the elimination of waste products. When these needs are not being adequately met, then our attention is directed toward meeting them. When these needs are strong, then we may no longer be able to control our behavior effectively and act in ways that we would prefer to, but rather we turn to activities that will tend to satisfy these needs. A starving man thinks primarily of food, and a sleepy man cannot keep his eyes open or focus his attention upon what is going on around him. Usually we accept these needs as realities of life, and we seldom feel guilty when we devote time and energy to meeting them. We accept them as part of being human. We don't expect ourselves to act as intelligently or as effectively when they are in an extreme state of deprivation as we do when they are reasonably satisfied.

The commonsense approach of many households to the effect that father should always be approached with problems after he has eaten rather than before is usually a wise one. When we are very hungry or very tired, we are not ready to be effective in helping others. We will tend to be more irritable and we will tend to oversimplify the situation to a greater degree than when we are less tired and less hungry. We will act in haste because of our own needs that require satisfaction and be less attentive to the needs of others.

When our needs are physical in nature, we are usually more accepting of them and more realistic about the impact they will have on our thinking and behavior than we are about our psychological needs. Frequently we tend to be unaware of the extent to which psychological needs are influencing our behavior. As a matter of fact, psychological needs are less well understood than physical needs; they are also more complicated in that they frequently involve our relationships with other people. These two factors probably account for the fact that they interfere with our attempts to help others much more than do physical needs and much more than we realize.

There is no one list of psychological needs that is accepted by all authorities. Hence we will not try to present a list of all psychological needs, and that is not even necessary for our purposes. What is important is that we recognize that psychological needs as well as physical needs affect our behavior. When we have been unsuccessful in obtaining some satisfaction for our psychological needs, then these needs will tend to dominate our thinking and behavior and we will be less able to be of real help to others. We will be in danger of responding more on the basis of our own needs than the needs of the person we are trying to help. Psychological needs include, among others, needs to organize our experiences in a meaningful way, to feel secure and adequate, to feel important and worthwhile, and to love and be loved.

A CASE ILLUSTRATION

Let us look at one example in some detail. Helping others can be a way of helping ourselves to feel important. The good feeling that we have when helping someone may reflect a satisfaction of our own need to be important. We want to be looked up to, respected by others. If we feel unimportant, overlooked, and rejected, then we may try to bolster our self-esteem by helping someone. We feel important when we see that the other individual needs us; we feel important when we see that we are making a contribution to his life. His "thanks," the look he gives us, makes it worth the effort. To some extent, this is a natural, normal, healthy response to helping others, and it can make helping others satisfying. We are not going to be less effective in helping others just because we enjoy it and feel important and useful in our helping activities.

But we can also become too interested in the importance that we feel and lose sight of the other person's need to feel important. Once having experienced this feeling of importance, we can be reluctant to let it go. We can unwittingly foster the other individual's need for our help; rather than help him to cope with his own problems, we may foster his turning to us for help beyond the point where this is beneficial to him. In brief, because of the strength of our own need to feel important, we may become dependent upon the individual we are trying to help; we become unable to let him go because to do so would be to give up the feeling of importance that we have gained from the relationship. We have perhaps unwittingly added to his difficulties rather than helped him.

Mr. Harris works in an office with many fellow workers. There is a great deal of work to be done, much of it of a similar nature, and many fellow employees work at essentially the same task. Mr. Harris at times feels like a small cog in a big machine, rather unimportant and of no special significance. He is not an aggressive person and he takes part in few activities or clubs. He has a wife and two children and spends most of his leisure hours at home. Under the gentle persuasion of a neighbor, he agreed to help with a Scout troop. A warm person who really likes people although he finds them a little frightening, Mr. Harris quickly became rather popular with the boys in the troop. He found this activity of helping the boys very satisfying and enjoyable after some initial anxiety, and he gradually became quite enthusiastic over it. He found himself making more and more suggestions, doing more and more of the planning, and making more and more of the decisions. The boys liked him, and he did have good suggestions and he did make sound decisions. He was important in the boys' eyes and he felt it; the feeling was good. He gave more and more of his time, gave the boys more special sessions in hiking and camping, and so on. He found himself feeling somewhat lonely and disappointed when the boys had another activity planned for the weekend and were unable to go hiking or camping. Soon he found himself wondering if the boys really appreciated his efforts; after all, he was giving up his weekends to help them and they weren't showing up regularly any more. Slight feelings of resentment now began to arise from time to time, and gradually he found himself losing interest. What had happened?

Many things had happened. At this point let us examine just one possibility. Mr. Harris, who did not feel especially important in this world, had reluctantly become involved in helping the local Scouts. Then he had found an importance he had perhaps never known, or had at least not experienced for a long time. For a while this worked in everyone's favor; because he again felt important, he looked forward to his Scouting activity, he was responsive to the boys' needs, and it was a two-way helping relationship, as the best helping relationships often are. But he was not aware of what was going on in himself; he was not aware of his own needs that were being met, nor that they soon became the dominant factor in the situation. He began to make more and more demands on the boys' time, to take over their activities and planning and decision-making processes. The boys then began backing off, and Mr. Harris felt hurt and rejected. Unwittingly, the motive to help others had been unduly influenced by his need to feel important and wanted and needed. Without meaning to do so, he had let his own need for importance come before the boys' needs to feel important. As this happened, his influence on the boys became less and less a helpful one and more and more a negative one in which, without realizing it, he was robbing them of their opportunity to feel important.

When we really want to be of help to another, we must continually be aware of the extent to which our own needs are determining our behavior and whether or not they are interfering with our intention to be of help. Helping others to help themselves requires that we accept our own needs as well as the needs of others. Maintenance needs must be met if we and others are to be free to continue to grow and develop. In general, the stronger our own unmet needs the less able we will be to attend to the needs of others. It is only when we have our own needs, both physical and psychological, under reasonable and comfortable control through accepting them and not denying them that we can direct our complete energies to helping another.

RELATION OF FEELINGS AND THOUGHTS TO ACTION

As human beings we all have feelings and emotions. We react with feelings as well as understand with reason. Frequently our feelings influence our thinking and reasoning with the effect that we are less able to make intelligent decisions and act realistically. We very frequently confuse some crucial differences between our feelings and thoughts, on the one hand, and our actions on the other. As humans we cannot escape taking responsibility for our actions and we cannot escape the fact of having feelings and thoughts. Our actions are to be controlled appropriately, and our feelings and thoughts are to be accepted graciously. Accepting and being aware of our thoughts and feelings, whatever they might be, does not mean that we are going to give them expression in action. On the contrary, the greater our awareness and acceptance of our thoughts and feelings, whatever they might be, the more able we will be to control our actions and to prevent our impulses from unduly influencing what we do and say. The mature person is able to experience fully and permissively, without censure, his thoughts and feelings and to control his actions with regard to the appropriateness of time, place, and circumstance. The possibility of appropriately controlled actions *without* awareness of feelings and thoughts is far more remote than the possibility of controlled actions *with* awareness of feelings and thoughts.

We hurt others primarily by what we say and do, by our behavior and our actions, rather than by our thoughts and feelings. To feel mad toward someone and to think of hitting him, and to be aware of this feeling and thought and then not to hit him is to be in control of ourselves. To feel mad toward someone and to want to hit him, and to be unaware of this desire, leaves us less in control of ourselves with greater possibility that we may hit him indirectly through "accident" or a "slip of the tongue."

It is our fear of our feelings and thoughts that gives us the real difficulty, not our feelings and thoughts by themselves. When we are afraid our feelings and thoughts will run away with us and overwhelm us if we acknowledge they are there, and when in response to our fear and anxiety we try to pretend we have no such feelings, then we are really in danger of being overwhelmed by them. Just because we fool ourselves into thinking that we do not have feelings does not mean that we do not have them; we have only succeeded in pushing the feelings out of our conscious control. The price of pretending that we do not have thoughts and feelings that we do have is very high, for it usually impairs our capacity to find life personally satisfying and to be productive in our work. It also increases the possibility that we will unduly interfere in the lives of others, even under the intent of wanting to help them. When positive thinking involves pretending that we do not have honest feelings and thoughts that are present, then we are usually just trying to run away from ourselves.

There is a place for the positive thinking, however, which leads us to have faith in our capacity to experience our feelings and thoughts and also control our behavior and actions. Every day we have many feelings and thoughts which we would never express in action. What male has not noticed a pretty female and thought thoughts that he has controlled as far as actions are concerned? What mother can honestly say that there haven't been times when she would really have liked to let Junior have it, but that she checked the impulse appropriately as far as her actions were concerned? What person has not looked in a window and wished for an object inside, but refrained from breaking the window and taking the object? We all have feelings, and frequently strong ones, that we are able to control appropriately. Just as we have learned to control many of our feelings, denying some from action and expressing others under appropriate conditions, we can also learn to control other thoughts and feelings that might frighten us because we find them unacceptable.

The extent to which we fool ourselves has a great influence upon how helpful we can be to others. The parent who cannot accept his own sexual feelings will be of little help to the teen-ager who is struggling with his or hers. The youth group leader who is unable to accept his own capacity for feeling hostile will be of little help to the delinquent who is ineffectively struggling with his own hostilities. The father who is frightened by tender feelings toward other males will find himself increasingly unable to give his growing son the tenderness he needs. The person who finds himself unlovable and frightening because of his inability to accept his own feelings and thoughts will tend to find others unlovable and frightening. To love our neighbors as ourselves, we must be able to love ourselves. To love ourselves we must know and accept ourselves.

UNDERSTANDING VALUE SYSTEMS

As human beings we all have values and beliefs concerning right and wrong, good and bad, that we learned when we were very young. These values will be the same as those held by some people, they will be similar to those held by some, and they will be different and even contradictory to those held by still others. If we are going to help others, then we must be careful not to assume that they think the same as we do about right and wrong. They can be doing what they think is "right" and have learned is "right" just as we are doing what we think is "right." Thus, people can behave differently and each can be convinced that he is behaving rightly. And they both can be considered from their own value system.

If we want to help others we must first attempt to understand their value systems and accept that it is possible that they are acting in good faith with their own values even if they are different from ours. We do not have to accept their values as our own, and we do not have to approve of their values; but we must accept the fact that they hold the values they do if we want to understand and help them.

Second, value systems can and do change. How much they will change depends upon several factors. It depends upon the intensity with which the values were learned and with which they are held as well as the awareness and desire of the individual to question his own values. Just as "you can take the boy out of the farm but you can't take the farm out of the boy," we probably seldom are able to change completely our values and live comfortably with values strange and different from those we learned while growing up.

Our "rights" and "wrongs" are frequently an accident of the time and place of our childhood. But it is possible for us to become aware of our values, to question them, and even to change them to some extent if this is deemed desirable. Values that cannot stand questioning are probably not worth having. Many times it is not the value system that will not hold up under questioning; it is the individual. Hence we should go very easy in questioning the values of others; it is generally best to let individuals question their own values and beliefs themselves. We can often be of most help in this respect by our own example. If we are comfortable in questioning our own values and beliefs, then others will be more likely to question their own.

Our society itself is very unclear as to its own values. Conflicts between value systems are rather characteristic of modern, complex civilizations. One example of such a conflict in values in our culture is that between the Christian ethic and the code of the competitive marketplace. The businessman in a competitive society finds it very difficult to survive and prosper in his business by acting on such values as "the meek will inherit the earth" and "do unto others as you would have them do unto you." Another area of conflict is seen in attitudes toward sexual feelings and behavior. Young persons are taught that sexual feelings must be controlled and sexual intercourse is to be engaged in only after marriage, yet they are stimulated continually by movies and advertisements that emphasize sexuality. If we are going to understand and help people, then we cannot ignore the value conflicts that are internalized by them from the conflicting value systems of the society in which they live. To pretend that conflicts in values do not exist because they make us uncomfortable and because we have no quick and easy way of resolving them is seldom, if ever, helpful.

There is no quick and easy answer to resolving the difficulties of mankind that occur as a consequence of different and sometimes conflicting value systems. We do know, however, that people do not exist in a vacuum and that we must recognize the importance of the values of their cultures and subcultures if we are to help more than harm. We know also that it is seldom helpful to take a rigid self-righteous, moralistic, and authoritarian attitude toward the beliefs and values of others.

Let us also not forget that our own concern with helping others to help themselves is a value belief, hopefully one that has been questioned and found sound. In fact, much of this book is concerned with examining the question as to why we want to or should help others help themselves. If we want to function with as much self-awareness as possible, then we must accept the fact that we, also, are not immune to our culture and its conflicting values and that, at times, we will find a conflict of interest between our helping intentions and other intentions and motives. We must accept that we, also, are human and that we will not always function in a helpful manner, even sometimes when we want to do so. At other times we will, hopefully with full awareness of what we are doing, purposefully function in a non-helpful or even harmful and exploiting way toward others. To accept our own varied motives and behaviors is to increase our sensitivity to the varied motives and behaviors of others, and to increase the likelihood of our being helpful when we want to be.

If we are going to be realistic, we must also accept the fact that some people will feel differently about helping others. A few individuals will be found who do not even pay lip service to this value; many individuals will be found who do not go beyond lip service to it. We may not agree with them, but it would only be folly on our part to pretend that such people do not exist. More frequently we will find that others are also interested in helping, but that disagreement arises with respect to what would be most helpful and who should function when and how in the helping process.

In helping others to help themselves we are often concerned with others examining their own values, and with their developing some understanding as to how they came to have such values. We are concerned with others becoming aware of the values they hold, and with their modifying these values, if need be, to be more in keeping with the kind of person that they want to become. We are concerned with helping individuals to become mature enough to say, "This is what I believe and these are the values that guide my decisions and behavior," rather than functioning in a blind, automatic way with no realization of what they believe or why they believe it.

Helping others does not mean making them over in our own image so that they will have the same values as we do. This is an easy fact to grasp intellectually, but it is difficult for most of us to let it seep into our deeper feelings. In our own needs to be right and to be important and to be liked we sometimes confuse our own perceptions of when we are most helpful. Many times we are most helpful when the person we are trying to help decides and behaves in a way that we, ourselves, would not decide or behave. What is right for him might not necessarily be right for us. We encourage others to do what *they* think is right, and then we become disturbed when they do not do what *we* think is right. It is tempting to observe, with the prophet of Ecclesiastes, that "all is vanity." The line between wanting to help and wanting to convert is sometimes very thin.

Even professional helpers are frequently plagued by frustrations arising from this conflict. The physician who diagnoses and informs a patient that he has a heart condition and must change his style of life often feels that he has not really helped the patient if the patient does not act on the basis of this advice. The patient may, after considering all aspects of the situation, decide that he prefers a shorter, more active life rather than a longer, more passive life. If this decision has been reached in a relatively rational manner, without ignoring or denying relevant realistic factual information, then has the physician's functioning been unhelpful? How far does one's helping responsibility to another go? Do we intervene at the verbal level, or do we go beyond and intervene actively and against another's will? We find ourselves continually struggling with the ancient question and meaning of, "Am I my brother's keeper?" And, if so, to what extent?

In our scientific world this same problem is seen in another context. A high school senior has consulted the school counselor for information about his chances to succeed in college. He is given a battery of tests and, on the solid and valid basis of what others have done in College X who have achieved scores like his on this test, he is told that he has only 5 chances out of 100 in succeeding in College X. However, he is also told that he has 80 chances out of 100 in succeeding in College Y. All available information, obtained and analyzed in accordance with the best methods known, supports this same conclusion with respect to the student's chances for success in College X and in College Y. The student, after considering everything in several sessions with his counselor, decides to enroll in College X anyway.

The counselor feels frustrated and questions whether he has been of any help to this student. If we mean has he enabled the student to make and act on the decision that would seem best by objective judgment and the best of modern knowledge, then the counselor would have to be considered a failure. Unfortunately, too many counselors experience just this feeling by viewing their role in this way. If, however, we consider it important that an individual make his own decision and take responsibility for his own actions and decisions, after considering rationally all relevant information available, then can we consider the counselor a failure? Seeking and understanding factual information and the probabilities of success does not mean that the individual should always decide in favor of the best odds. Some will want to risk more for certain goals that they consider more important than others. Whether we will support them in their decisions, even though these decisions are different from those we would make, depends many times more on ourselves and our own values than on the values and needs of the person we are trying to help. If we have strong needs for security ourself, then we would have decided differently; and, if we have not carefully thought through our role as a helping person, then we might feel frustrated and a failure as a helping person.

It cannot be stressed too much that the satisfaction we will experience in helping others to help themselves, as well as our skill in this endeavor, will depend to a large extent upon how carefully we have thought through exactly what it is we are trying to do in our efforts to help others. We will measure ourselves in relation to the goals and expectations we have set for ourselves. There is no fixed yardstick that we can all agree upon for this task, and there is no one set of goals that we would all agree upon as goals of the helping process. Each of us, however, has to develop a set of values and goals that he can live with, and this includes values and goals about helping others for those who want to be both realistic and comfortable in this activity.

THE INTELLIGENCE FACTOR

As human beings we all have certain intellectual capacities and abilities. However, we are not equal with respect to our capacities and abilities. Just as we differ physically, we also differ with respect to our intelligence. We differ not only with respect to what we have learned and what we have achieved, but also with respect to our capacity to learn and to achieve. We differ with respect to our capacity to behave intelligently, to reason and to think, to memorize and to comprehend, to visualize spatial relations and to perceive complexities in the world around us.

Our capacity to function intelligently is dependent upon many factors. Each of us has limits to our potential capacities and aptitudes which are probably determined by heredity and by constitutional factors. The degree to which we will actualize our capacities, however, is determined to a large extent by environmental opportunities and conditions as well as by our motivation to use and develop our capacities.

People not only differ from each other in their general level of intelligence and in their potentials for intelligent functioning, but each individual also differs from time to time in his own level of intelligent behavior. No one consistently functions at peak capacity all the time. People are not machines, and we cannot set ourselves at a certain level and maintain that level of functioning consistently. Under special conditions, such as fatigue or intoxication, we will not function as intelligently as we might otherwise. When we are emotionally disturbed, when we are confronted with a stressful situation that makes us very anxious, or when we are in deep conflict about something, we are usually not capable of functioning as intelligently as at other times.

If we are to be realistic in our efforts to help others to help themselves, we must accept the facts that people differ with respect to their capacities and that each individual differs from time to time in his own capacity to function intelligently. Some people have greater capacity to assume responsibility for themselves and to solve their problems than other people. Even a person who is usually very capable and responsible in his behavior may become, in a crisis situation, temporarily seriously impaired in his capacity to help himself. There is no simple test that will tell us precisely how capable an individual is of responding intelligently and to what degree he can be expected to help himself. Although it is difficult to make these judgments, it is not impossible to achieve a fair degree of accuracy in doing so. Certainly there will be many times when we err; but if we are afraid of making a mistake, then we would forever do nothing. Every day, as a matter of fact, we make judgments about other peoples' capacities and their potential for intelligent functioning. Without usually being consciously aware of it, we have been practicing this since childhood with almost everyone we know. It would be impossible to live and interact with others without making judgments and having opinions about their capacities.

Sometimes people will say that they do not make judgments about others because that is not nice or because they do not have the training to do so. Such people are only fooling themselves, a fact usually apparent to others. There is a difference between being judgmental toward others in a moralistic and self-righteous manner and making judgments about others. Making judgments about others does not mean that we have to be moralistically judgmental toward them. Even when we do not make conscious judgments about others, we unconsciously do so and form impressions of others that influence our attitudes toward them. It is true that most people have not had formalized, technical training in making judgments about the intelligence of others; even professionals who have had such training have a healthy respect for how little we actually know about what intelligence is or how to measure it.

The situation is similar to making judgments about the physical health of others. We all do this, day in and day out, both with ourselves and with others. Most adults have learned to recognize many cues that suggest someone is not feeling well. We have all participated in making judgments as to the seriousness of a symptom and as to whether or not a physician should be consulted. Just as we all make judgments about the health of others without pretending to be physicians, we also make judgments about the intelligence and capacities of others without pretending to be psychologists. To function otherwise would not only be ignoring our responsibilities in interpersonal relations, but it would also probably be impossible.

The danger is not in making such judgments, but in not doing so responsibly and consciously with full awareness of our limitations in doing so. Life, after all, is continually a process of deciding and acting when we are never as prepared as we would like to be.

Mental illness and mental retardation are terms that are still confusing to many people. They do not mean the same thing, but refer to two different phenomena. When an individual experiences difficulty in coping with his feelings and emotions, we say that he is emotionally disturbed. This can be of a very mild nature or it can be very severe. We all become mildly emotionally disturbed from time to time, much as we have a common cold from time to time. Under greater stress, whether this is from factors outside ourselves or from factors inside ourselves, we may become moderately disturbed or even severely emotionally disturbed. When an individual is severely emotionally disturbed, then we say that he is mentally ill. A mentally ill person needs professional treatment, and the goal of this treatment is usually to enable him to return to his former condition before he became mentally ill. Sometimes, of course, it is possible to help the individual attain a state of mental health beyond that which he experienced previously, while at other times it is possible only to minimize the effects of the mental illness. The treatment procedure may be short or it may be long, and it may involve weekly interviews with a psychotherapist or it may involve hospitalization.

Mental illness refers to disturbances of emotions and feelings, which may be reflected and displayed in disordered thoughts and ideas. Mental retardation refers to a general level of intelligence considerably below the average level of intelligence. The individual usually develops mentally at a slower rate and to a lesser extent than the average person. With few exceptions, it is not possible to treat or correct a condition of severe mental retardation so that the individual will have average intelligence. Severe mental retardation is usually irreversible, meaning that the damage or lack of development cannot be undone, while mental illness is usually reversible, meaning that the disorder can usually be treated or corrected to some extent at least. Another way of stating this would be to say that mental illness is usually a temporary condition whereas mental retardation is usually a permanent condition. Thus mental illness is usually considered a medical and psychological problem, while mental retardation is usually considered an educational and training problem.

About 3 or 4 per cent of the population of the United States is mentally retarded; this is about the same proportion of individuals who would be called gifted or extremely intelligent. It is important to note, however, that there are many differences among mentally retarded people. Some are borderline mentally retarded and can benefit from special education classes in the public school system. These individuals, with proper training and guidance, will be able to function semi-independently and will be able to assume active employment in unskilled and semiskilled jobs as adults. Others, however, are severely retarded and will probably always need care and supervision. They will not be able to hold jobs in the general community, although they will be able to take care of some of their personal needs and perhaps help with household tasks. These individuals are sometimes called "trainable retarded," while the borderline group is called "educable retarded." A small group of mentally retarded individuals will be so severely retarded that they will require continual bed care; these individuals usually also have many physical impairments and are primarily medical and nursing problems.

A person who is mentally ill is not necessarily mentally retarded, and a person who is mentally retarded is not necessarily mentally ill. Very bright people as well as retarded people may become mentally ill. Mentally ill people may sometimes also be mentally retarded. The majority of mentally ill people, however, are not mentally retarded, and the majority of mentally retarded people are not mentally ill.

THE LEARNING PROCESS

In discussing needs, values, and other fundamental aspects of human behavior, frequent mention has been made of learning. Many of our needs and probably all of our values and beliefs are learned. That is, we were not born with them and we did not inherit them; rather, we acquired them largely in interaction with others. The learning process is very basic to human functioning, and there is some evidence that learning starts before birth. Only a very small part of our learning experiences occur in a formal classroom. In fact, many of the things we learned that now play a large part in determining our behavior were learned in childhood before we entered school. Many of our strongest values and beliefs, our prejudices and biases, our tendency to trust or not to trust others, our capacity to love, and our attitudes toward ourselves had their firm beginnings in learning experiences that occurred before we entered school. Because of our immaturity at the time, and our capacity to forget, we often act as if we were "born that way" and feel that these characteristics could not have been learned.

We are continually learning, day in and day out, and to some extent attitudes and values that we learned earlier are modified by later experiences. People are similar to a river that is always changing as we look at it, yet never changing in other ways. It is precisely because of our capacity to change and to mature and to learn greater competencies and more effective ways of living that it is realistic to want to help others help themselves. Yet at the same time it would be folly not to recognize that we all have limits to the extent that we can change. Hence helping others to help themselves is the art of learning when to step in and do for another and when to step back and let another do for himself. It is the art of learning to expect neither too little nor too much from the person we are trying to help. Through learning experiences, both formal and informal, we can refine and increase our skill in helping others to help themselves. There is very little, if anything, that any adult thinks or does that is not influenced by both present and past learning experiences.

The learning process has been studied for many years very intensively by both psychologists and educators. Although it is true that the more we learn the more we become aware of how little we know, some general principles have been formulated about learning that can be helpful to us. In very simple terms we can say that the most effective learning usually occurs when (1) there is a need, want, desire, drive, (2) the person becomes alert and attentive to the world around him, (3) the person does something, (4) the person gets rewarded in some way for his action or decision. These are the four most important factors in an effective learning situation, and they have very great implication for our efforts to help others.

The helping experience is basically a learning experience. It is usually most effective when the individual wants help, when he gives his attention to the helping process and to the problem that confronts him, when he does something about solving his problem or conflict, and when he feels rewarded by a greater feeling of confidence, achievement or satisfaction. To the extent that any of these aspects of the process are lacking, then the effectiveness of the helping relationship is usually impaired.

If we push our help on someone who is not ready for it and does not want it, or if we wait until he no longer needs it, then our helping effort can be in vain. The timing of helping efforts is of crucial importance; help given too soon or too late can be equally ineffective. The most opportune time to help is usually when the individual himself feels the need for help. The parent who, from her own anxiety, presses information on the preadolescent about boy-girl relationships before the preadolescent views this as a significant aspect of life will frequently meet with only a rebuff. The parent who waits until the adolescent has become overburdened with boy-girl relationships, or the lack of them, and has developed strong defensive and protective reactions, will have waited too long. The time to help the adolescent with support and understanding of boy-girl relationships is when he or she first begins to consider these relationships important, and, directly or indirectly, strives to obtain some guidelines and support.

If our timing is good, then we will usually have the individual's attention. With adolescents this may mean, of course, that they will not always acknowledge that they are listening to what is being said, even when they are. It is sometimes very easy to think that someone is not noticing what we are saying or doing, and then get irritated with them. This usually only drives them away from us. If our timing is right, our words will seldom fall on deaf ears or our actions on blind eyes, even when the ears and eyes seem turned in other directions.

The third aspect of the helping process viewed as a learning situation is very difficult for some people. It is difficult because we must often control and curb our own eagerness or anxiety and let the other person decide or do for himself. We must be prepared for the other person to make errors in judgment and to make mistakes in action, while at the same time holding firm to our faith that he will come through successfully on his own. It is a rare person who always learns and performs successfully the first time; yet how often we become irritated with others when they do not do just this. This is the time when our moral support is needed, not our actions or decisions. Our own confidence in ourselves as a helping person, as well as our confidence in the other person, is necessary here. The mother robin serves as a good example: baby robins, sooner or later, must try their own wings. The moment of truth cannot be avoided forever.

The reward, the fourth aspect of a good learning experience, consists in the increased self-esteem and confidence and satisfaction the individual experiences, as well as the decreased fear and anxiety, when his decisions and actions bring him closer to solving his problem or reaching his goal. If the individual has made a choice in decision or action that has been ineffective, or even a flat failure, then moral support to reconsider and to try again is needed. This does not mean glossing over the fact that the choice was an ineffective one, or that the attempt was a failure; on the contrary, it means an acceptance of this result in a realistic manner. As stated earlier, it is only realistic to expect that more than one attempt will have to be made to solve most problems. Overprotection at this step can be very crippling emotionally, undermining the individual's self-confidence and self-esteem. It is when he senses our own easy acceptance of the poor attempt and the expectation that it will proceed better next time, as if this were just the natural course of events, that he receives renewed strength to make the next attempt.

The helping person himself will experience these same four aspects of the learning process. He must want to help others, he must be alert and attentive to what helps and what does not help, he must do or be someting, and his reward will be the satisfaction of having been a positive influence in another's efforts to help himself. The latter two points merit special comment. What we are is as important, and many times more important, than what we do or say when we want to help someone else. The most helpful act of all many times is the mere presence of someone who has faith in our capacities to help ourselves; they do not have to do anything, but their act of being, their mere presence, is all important.

If we really are interested in helping others to feel more adequate and self-confident, then we must not look for, or expect, verbal thanks or acknowledgment of our help. The individual will feel, and perhaps honestly so, that he did it himself. To look for our reward in his acknowledgment of our help would be to want to diminish the experience for him, to want to decrease his self-esteem ever so slightly. Way down deep, most of us cherish the dream and illusion of being independent; we basically do not like having to take help. To help someone and then to expect gratitude is not really to help, not in the sense of helping others to help themselves. Perhaps this is why helping others to help themselves can be viewed as the most difficult and most mature relationship of which a human is capable. It is, for most of us, an ideal to aspire to. We can gauge our success by how close we come to it, not by the audacity of thinking we can consistently achieve it.

3

More About
Human Behavior

▶We humans are a very ingenious species, much more so than we realize. Our technological achievements are significant tributes to our energy, intelligence, and resourcefulness. Great as our achievements have been in coping with the world around us, however, they are at least equalled by our resourcefulness in fooling ourselves. The current state of man's technological capacity to destroy himself through superbombs has its counterpart in his capacity to fool and deceive himself concerning his own being. Our accomplishments in distortion are indeed wondrous to behold, although often pathetically tragic.

ANXIETY

One of the mixed blessings of being human is the capacity to experience anxiety. Under conditions of stress we tend to react with anxiety. The stress of uncertainty, the stress of feeling helpless, the stress of having conflicts, the stress of having feelings and thoughts which we do not want to accept, as well as many other conditions, all tend to arouse anxiety. Anxiety is an uncomfortable reaction, and we tend to mobilize our resources to reduce the anxiety. We try to escape the feeling of anxiety as much as possible. In our efforts to avoid it, we frequently react in ways which interfere with our capacity to be mature and responsible. We react in ways which tend to reduce our immediate anxiety, but which frequently create the conditions that will lead to greater anxiety later, or to less effective functioning, or to impaired capacity to find satisfaction with life. Many times we relieve our own anxiety only at the expense of someone else.

In resolving conflicts and relieving anxiety we often make use of a variety of techniques which have been called defense mechanisms. They are defensive because they represent our attempt to defend ourselves against anxiety by fooling ourselves, rather than by tolerating the anxiety and taking realistic steps to alleviate it and change the conditions giving rise to it. We resist the change that might be necessary in our own way of functioning, and we try to defend ourselves by fooling ourselves. We become defensively concerned with avoiding anxiety rather than focusing our attention upon the realities involved. When we function in primarily a defensive manner, then we are usually behaving neurotically.

We all function defensively at times. We differ only in the extent and the manner in which we function defensively. Some of us make more use of some defense mechanisms, and others of us make more use of other defense mechanisms. We each differ from time to time, also, in the degree to which we function in this manner. And we seldom use just one defense mechanism, but more often use several.

An important characteristic of defensive functioning is that it is unconscious. We are not aware of what we are doing when we are in the process of using defense mechanisms. That is why they are successful in relieving us from experiencing conscious anxiety. Sometimes we can recognize later that we were functioning defensively, or someone else may call it to our attention. Then our defense techniques become less effective, although we may continue to use them to fool ourselves on a conscious level. At such times they cannot be considered true defense mechanisms, but they can still enable us to distort and to gloss over reality.

Ten common defense mechanisms will be discussed, although there are actually many more. In discussing them it is important to remember that (1) they are used unconsciously, (2) they are used by all of us and, in moderation, are normal although not necessarily healthy, and (3) they are ways in which we distort reality and fool ourselves to avoid anxiety.

REPRESSION

The mechanism of repression is probably the most fundamental and common of all the defense mechanisms. Through repression we prevent feelings or thoughts that would be unacceptable to us from becoming conscious. It is as if we short-circuit, as it were, unpleasant impulses and ideas so that we will not have to recognize and accept that we have them. The mechanism of repression can be thought of as a kind of screening device which we are unaware of that functions to keep painful material from coming to our conscious awareness. It is a special kind of forgetting, although the forgetting occurs only on a conscious level. Through repression we avoid anxiety by not letting ourselves become aware of what would be anxiety-producing to us if we were aware of it.

Under severe conditions of stress, such as being in an accident or fighting on a battlefield, some individuals will repress the entire incident. They will "forget" everything that happened because to remember what occurred would be too threatening and anxiety-producing for them. More commonly, as children many of us learned to repress feelings and thoughts which we were taught were "bad" as we were growing up. Thus, some individuals are unable to tolerate the thought of any hostile or angry feelings toward their parents. They have been taught that such feelings are "bad' and have learned to fool themselves about having any such feelings because they do not want to think of themselves as "bad." In normal parent-child relationships hostile and angry feelings will occur from time to time and will be worked off in acceptable ways, or merely tolerated and dissipated in time. When we repress our feelings, we put them beyond our conscious control. We do not do away with the feeling; we merely deceive ourselves as to our reactions. Probably all of us do this to some extent without any severe effects. However, when we repress to an extreme degree, then we impair our capacity to cope effectively with reality. We become less effective in our work and less satisfied in our relationships with others. We use much of our energy repressing, and have less energy to use for constructive purposes.

Many times when we feel "blue" or "moody" with no apparent reason, we have merely repressed the reasons for our feelings. We have repressed the feeling or thought that causes our depressive feeling, so we are unaware of why we feel "blue." Very frequently we tend to feel depressed when we have repressed hostile feelings that are unacceptable to us. Under certain conditions we may remember material that we have repressed, or some of the material may come through to consciousness in disguised form. This often happens in dreams or under the effects of alcohol or when we are fatigued; it happens when our conscious control is not as vigilant and effective as it usually is.

An individual who tends to use the mechanism of repression consistently to an undue degree as a way of avoiding anxiety and conflict will be impaired in his capacity to be of help to others. First, he will be using considerable energy defending himself against his own thoughts and feelings so that he will be less free to respond to others. Second, he will be anxious and uncomfortable in helping others who are struggling with problems that are similar to his own. He will tend to gloss over feelings and thoughts that they have which would make him uncomfortable because they are too similar to the feelings and thoughts that he has repressed. For example, some adults find it difficult to establish fruitful helping relationships with adolescents because many of the conflicts that adolescents want to verbalize and discuss are too similar to conflicts the adults have experienced and repressed.

Third, feelings and impulses that have been repressed have not "disappeared" and "gone away"; on the contrary, they are still striving for expression and frequently find expression in action in disguised form. The individual who represses his hostility, for example, is very prone to make "slips of the tongue" which are cutting and painful to others without being aware of it or despite his conscious intentions to do the opposite. He is in danger of putting his foot in his mouth, so to speak, and behaving in a hostile manner toward others before he is aware of what he is doing.

No one likes to think that he is prejudiced, yet it is probably a very rare person who is able to grow to adulthood without acquiring some prejudices along the way. As children we learn many of the prejudiced values of others and in unawareness make them our own. When we learn later that we should not feel hostile toward others because of their race or religion, we many times tend to repress the feelings and thoughts we have learned. We do not want to be prejudiced, so we repress any thoughts or feelings of a prejudiced nature. But this does not mean they have "gone away"; if we have only repressed them, then they are very much with us and they will usually find their way into our thinking and acting without our being aware of their influence. It is probably more mature to recognize and to be aware of our feelings that might be prejudice more than anything else, and then to try and change them or at least control them when we are deciding and acting.

RATIONALIZATION

The mechanism of rationalization is very common and probably very well known. Through the process of rationalization we convince ourselves that what we are saying or doing is reasonable and justifiable. Through rationalization we give our hopes and fears, our wishes and needs, the cloak of logical respectability and approval. We find reasons and excuses to justify our behavior. It is important to remember that when we are really rationalizing we are not aware of what we are doing. When we comment to ourselves that we are rationalizing, then we are in effect no longer rationalizing in a pure sense. We usually become aware of our rationalizations only after we have behaved on the basis of them. What seemed reasonable at the time frequently is seen later as rationalization born out of fear or wishful thinking.

Most people, at some time or other, have probably rationalized either not helping someone or actively interfering in another's life. At one extreme we find the parents who never help their child, rationalizing that "It is better that he learn to do it on his own," or "I'm just too busy now; that work at the office just can't wait," or "He should be able to do all his work at school," or "He wouldn't understand anyway, so why bother to explain to him?" At the other extreme we find the parent who continually forces his help upon his child, rationalizing that "It's all for his own good," or "He wouldn't be able to get it if I didn't help him," or "The teacher just doesn't give him the help he needs at school." The important point is that when we are rationalizing our helping behavior—or lack of it—toward others, then we are less likely to respond to what would be best for them and more likely to respond on the basis of our own anxieties and wishes.

It is very difficult to determine when our statements and thinking are valid reasons for making decisions regarding our behavior and when they are essentially rationalizations. Usually when we feel the urge to do something and then start trying to justify our behavior, we are rationalizing. When we find ourselves unusually touchy or irritable when someone questions our behavior, and when we feel a strong need to defend our behavior and justify it to others, then we will usually find ourselves engaging in rationalizations.

PROJECTION

Projection is the mechanism whereby we attribute to others feelings and thoughts which we find unacceptable in ourselves. Instead of accepting our own feelings, we may project them on to others and act as if they, not us, have the feelings. We tend to externalize our feelings and thoughts through this mechanism; that is, we function as if the unacceptable impulses were external to us and belonged to somebody else. In very severe cases, an individual may hallucinate and project his unacceptable impulses on to others who are not actually there; in such cases the person may "hear voices" and "see people" saying and doing things that he cannot tolerate in himself. More usually, however, we project on to others who are present and we tend to distort, mistrust, and misinterpret their motives and behavior. Thus, we may feel that they are mad at us when it is actually we who are mad at them. Or, as in the case of the rather cruel joke that is often told, the woman who cannot tolerate her own sexual feelings may think that every man she meets is making a pass at her; she believes it is the men that have the sexual feelings, not her.

To the extent that we project we will be impairing our capacity to be of help. Perhaps one of the most common forms of projection that occurs in helping behavior is when the helper projects his own anxiety on to the individual he is helping. This is seen frequently when young children and adults are involved in a stressful situation. There are many situations that adults, because of their past experiences or because of the reality of the situation, perceive as anxiety-producing and stressful but which children do not perceive as stressful. The adult then acts as if the child were anxious also; he projects his own anxiety on to the child and then endeavors to relieve the child's anxiety.

In this way adults often induce anxiety in children when the children would probably have experienced little or no anxiety in the situation if it were not for the adult's anxiety. This pattern is seen many times when a child has to go to the hospital, or to the dentist, or to take a test in school. This may also occur when the stressful situation is solely in the life of the adult. One way of coping with anxiety is to do something active. Many times parents will be anxious about something in their own lives, perhaps their marital relationship or a vocational situation, and in their efforts to cope with their own anxiety they will focus upon the child and drain their anxieties through becoming overly helpful and involved with their child's activities.

Often people who need help are unable to accept their feeling of helplessness and their need for help. They may project this feeling and need on to others and then try to help others. They may view everybody else as needing help rather than themselves. In this way they protect themselves from the anxiety that they would feel if they accepted their own need for help. They seek to help where help is not needed in order to fool themselves that it is others who need help and not themselves.

COMPENSATION

Through compensation we attempt to make up for what we feel are deficiencies, inadequacies, or defects in ourselves by intense striving and effort. This may be direct, in that we strive to overcome the defect, or it may be indirect, in that we ignore the defect and make up for it by emphasizing other characteristics. The defect or deficiency need not be real, in the sense that others would agree as to there being an actual defect, but it is real to the person who experiences it. In fact, deficiencies and inadequacies that we perceive in ourselves and experience as very embarrassing and painful are often not even noticed by others. Adolescents frequently display considerable compensatory behavior with respect to developing physical characteristics. The boy of fourteen who is seen by others as being normally healthy and well-muscled may feel himself that he is the original "ninety-nine pound weakling" and exert great energy and effort in weight lifting and exercising to develop his muscles. While one boy may compensate directly in this manner, another boy may compensate indirectly by ignoring and avoiding muscular activities and focusing his energies on becoming the best debater in school or the most knowledgeable authority on missiles or cars.

Compensatory activities can sometimes be very useful socially and lead to valuable achievements, as well as being potentially harmful and injurious to others at other times. A woman with no children of her own may compensate for this loss by volunteering her services to a home for children or to a youth camp. This can result in an ideal helping relationship wherein both she and the children find life more satisfying and meaningful, or it can result in a harmful relationship wherein the children are exploited, usually unconsciously, by the woman to meet her own needs. The quality of the intended helping relationship, whether it is indeed beneficial or harmful to the children, will depend considerably upon the extent to which the woman is aware and accepting of her own needs and able to control them appropriately so that she can respond to the children primarily on the basis of their needs. If she has totally repressed her own painful feelings associated with her lack of a child, and has no awareness that these feelings are important in determining her desire to help children, then she will be likely to relate unconsciously to the children more on the basis of her needs than theirs.

In a society where many men are employed in tasks that are relatively routine and which demand little in the way of traditional masculine attributes, such as strength and physical courage, some men will experience vague feelings of masculine inadequacy with concomitant needs to display to themselves and others that they are really "he-men" in the tradiitonal manner. Youth activities such as sports and camping may attract some men essentially as media through which they can express masculine urges. Here, again, good helping relationships do not require that the helper avoid meeting any of his own needs; this would be an unrealistic expectation and would only foster our fooling ourselves as to the complexity of our motives. Rather, it is important that the leader be sufficiently aware of the temptation to steal the show and display his own powers and skills so that he will be able to control such impulses and allow the boys to express their own capacities. It is frequently very easy for the youth leader to catch the most fish, climb the highest mountain, or shoot the most baskets under the impression that he is merely setting an example or giving an appropriate demonstration. Certainly providing good examples and sound demonstrations is important, but it is also important that this part not be overdone to the extent that it is demoralizing to those we are trying to help.

DENIAL

Through denial we protect ourselves from conflict, anxiety, and other unpleasant feelings and thoughts by ignoring or denying unpleasant aspects of reality. We do not see or face facts or problems that would be unpleasant. We act as if the unpleasant reality does not really exist, or that it will go away if we do not give it any attention. We focus our attention elsewhere and make frequent use of rationalization to justify our not attending to the problem at hand.

Unlike compensation, denial seldom serves any socially beneficial or productive purpose. On the contrary, it generally serves only to postpone our having to come to grips with the unpleasant reality; in the meantime, the unpleasant reality may have increased in its intensity so that it will be even more difficult to cope with later.

The child who convinces himself that his tooth doesn't hurt when he learns that this will mean a trip to the dentist's office is denying an unpleasant reality and usually only postponing an inevitable course of action. The parent who really wants to help his child will usually proceed, firmly but gently, with the dental appointment despite the child's denials and protests. The parent who, because he cannot tolerate the child's suffering at the thought of going to the dentist, does not follow through with the dental examination is only participating in the child's dental reaction. Such behavior on the part of the parent is usually well-meaning, but from the long-range perspective it can hardly be considered as ultimately helpful to the child's growth and development. Not only will the child suffer needlessly with prolonged toothaches, but perhaps more importantly the child has learned something about coping with his feelings and with unpleasant realities that is, in the long range, ineffective and an obstacle to mature functioning. The child has learned to deny and ignore unpleasant realities rather than how to cope with them and face them. His confidence in his own capacities to cope with adversity other than by running away has been undermined.

For many people it is an unpleasant reality that people need help at times. Rather than accepting this fact, they deny it and then become very aggravated and irritated when someone attempts to confront them with the reality of an individual's need for help.

This occurs frequently with respect to both our own need for help and the need of other individuals for help. The tendency to deny someone's need for help is usually greatest when we feel helpless to help them. We are often really denying the reality of our own helplessness many times when we are denying another's need for help. There are probably few parents who cannot search their memories and find some experiences in their own behavior that are examples of such denial behavior.

Adults are often impatient with the difficulties and conflicts of adolescents because the adolescents raise questions with which the adults feel helpless to cope. The adult tends to deny the reality of the adolescent's problem in the all too human, but nevertheless unrealistic, hope that it will go away if not given attention. Adolescence, in a blend of compulsivity and impulsivity, abounds with the search for truth and justice; in a naively courageous and wonderful manner the unanswerable questions are discussed with great energy. Adulthood, faced with unanswerable questions, tends to reply with a grand denial. The difficulty of establishing justice in a world that is basically neutral, the frustration of compromising ideals with practical considerations, the anxiety associated with perceiving one's helplessness when confronted with the unanswerable and the unknowable, and the fear of the breakthrough of impulses in a world demanding controlled behavior all leave the typical middle-aged adult ready to embrace denial with a speed that amazes even the adolescent.

Blatant, outright denial of another's need for help is less often encountered than a halfhearted denial supported by rationalization. Thus, we may be unable to totally deny that Johnny is experiencing difficulty in his relations with neighborhood children, but we support our denial with the statement that "it really isn't serious enough to get worried about and he will probably outgrow it anyway." Or we can rationalize that "the Scoutleader or the teacher will help him work out his difficulties; after all, that's what they are for." Unable to fool ourselves to the extent of denying the problem, we sometimes are able to deny our responsibility for doing anything about it. We can even, in our unconscious ingenuity, marshal the forces of repression, projection, denial, and rationalization and go on to make the bold pronouncement that Johnny really doesn't have a problem—it is the other children who have the problem. Now we have really taken ourselves off the spot.

There is a common misconception that worrying is bad and that people should not worry. Worry, like anxiety, has an important role in our personality functioning. There are times when some worrying, like some anxiety, is not only healthy but also helpful in that it serves to mobilize our resources to consider the problem and to do something about it. Worry and anxiety are unhealthy only when they are so persistent and so intense that they immobilize us and prevent us from going on to resolve the problem. There is probably no statement less helpful and more communicative of the fact that we either do not understand, or do understand and are afraid ourselves, than the plea, "Now don't worry, it will turn out all right in the end" to someone who, very realistically, does have something to worry about.

We also may accept another's need for help, but then deny the complexities of the situation in our eagerness to relieve our own anxieties and do something helpful. We tend to oversimplify the situation by jumping to a conclusion that it is due to such-and-such, overlooking the fact that most situations and problems are influenced by several factors or causes. If we act too impulsively on the basis of the first possible cause that comes to mind, then we can sometimes be more harmful than helpful. We are denying our capacities to consider the complexity of the situation or problem and to tolerate the fact that we will probably not know all the causes but will be better able to help for having considered at least some of the probable causes. Again, our use of denial is frequently related to the anxiety we experience in facing our limitations in a very complex world. Unfortunately, our use of denial usually serves only to increase our limitations.

FANTASY

In our fantasies we attempt to fulfill wishes and desires that are unmet in the world of reality. In our imagination and daydreams we find the fulfillment and become the kind of person that in the harsh light of reality is not forthcoming. Most of us engage in fantasy activity, and hopefully we find pleasure and satisfaction in our imaginary adventures. Fantasy activity not only permits an occasional escape from the world around us, but may also stimulate new ideas that can be used productively.

Fantasy activity becomes neurotic and an impairment to effective living only when it serves as a substitute for, and not a complement to, active achievement. If all we do is daydream about helping others, then we will not have accomplished much in the way of actually being helpful. Helping activities, like most other activities, are not always glamorous and adventurous. They can sometimes become dull and routine. The person who has served as a volunteer helper in the same setting for several years usually matures in his conception of himself as a helping person. What was once new and novel and exciting may have become commonplace and routine. A more mature conception of the need for his services as a volunteer helper is usually necessary if he is to continue in his activities. The grass will look greener elsewhere, usually in places with exotic names where one has never been. Many people find it easier to become enthusiastic about helping people far away rather than close at hand; the battlefields of life are always more appealing from a distance.

DISPLACEMENT

Through displacement we express our feelings, usually of hostility, toward an object or person other than the object or person who initially aroused the feelings. We usually shift our focus from the person who initially aroused our feelings to someone or something less threatening and safer for us. Many behavioral patterns known to most families involve some displacement, as when father has a tough session with his boss and then comes home and yells at his wife, or when mother is mad at father and takes it out on the children. Modern society is characterized by many roles and relationships that are highly structured and which demand considerable control of feelings and emotions on the part of the individual. This is especially true of most working relationships and social relationships outside the family. For better or worse, the family in our society often serves as a buffer zone and retreat where pent-up feelings displaced from other relationships are given expression.

Children are especially vulnerable as receivers of displaced feelings, probably because they are less capable of making demands for control of feelings on adults than are other adults. Children also activate, both consciously and unconsciously, painful feelings and experiences that adults have repressed with the consequence that adults may give vent to old feelings that are not proportionate to the present situation.

The individual who assumes a responsibility as a helping person, whether professionally as a teacher or social worker or on a volunteer basis as a Brownie leader or mental health aide, must be especially aware of any tendencies to displace feelings on others. There will be some days when we approach our helping relationships with considerably more than usual pent-up feelings of anger and frustration; if we are not at least aware of our feelings at such times, then we will be in danger of displacing them toward the individuals we might be trying to help. There are times when it is best just to acknowledge openly with those you are trying to help that you are not your usual self that day and that you might not really be able to help much. Strange as it might seem, just such an admission that we, also, are human and are affected by our own problems and feelings will frequently not only help protect us from displacing our feelings but will also be more helpful to others than anything else we might have done. At such times we are helping by the example that we show; we are saying, in effect, that it is all right to have problems and to let others know and to be upset about them at times.

Displacement also occurs on a more abstract level in combination with projection to result in what is called scapegoating. Minority groups are frequently the target of scapegoating; all blame is projected on to the minority group and then pent-up feelings of hostility are discharged on the group. More commonly, however, authority figures, "the administration" and "the system," serve as scapegoats for many people. Authority figures are common targets for displacement, especially from a distance and with the company of others, because many of our pent-up hostilities originated in our relations with people who were authority figures for us, including our parents, but at whom we were not supposed to get mad. "The administration," "the institution," "the front office," and "the system" are also frequent targets of scapegoating which are especially safe because they are impersonal.

Many helping activities are organized through special groups, agencies, institutions, and hospitals. When we function as a helping person in an organization, we must realize that how effective we will be in helping others to help themselves will be dependent, to some extent, upon the effectiveness of the organization. Care must be taken not to undermine the effectiveness of the organization through projecting blame on the organization and then displacing our irritations and hostilities toward the organization. This does not mean that the organization is always right, or that we should not be critical of it; it does mean that we should exercise discretion and judgment as to where we express such critical judgments. It does not help a boy to feel proud and important as a Boy Scout to hear his Scoutmaster sounding off about certain policies or actions taken by the central council, and it does not help a patient feel comfortable and secure in a hospital to hear helping people in the hospital gripe about administrative practices of the business office. Such feelings and criticisms should be expressed where they will be potentially influential and not harmful, usually to appropriate administrators or through appropriate committees and study groups.

REACTION FORMATION

Through reaction formation we doubly protect ourselves from impulses that are unacceptable to us first by repressing the impulse or desire and, second, by developing attitudes and engaging in actions that are just the opposite of those we have repressed. Although defense mechanisms operate without our conscious awareness of what is happening—that is why they are effective in preventing us from consciously experiencing conflict and anxiety— we do function in similar ways on a conscious level. Thus we can gain some understanding of reaction formation by reflecting upon a similar process that occurs more or less consciously.

When we repress an idea or a feeling, we are not aware that we are repressing; when we suppress an idea or feeling, we are at least vaguely consciously aware of what we are doing. When we suppress a thought we are usually doing what is commonly called "pushing it to the back of our mind." There are times when we will try and push a thought or feeling to the back of our mind, as it were, or suppress it, because it is unpleasant for us to think about. When we also then act or think in just the opposite way, we are doing something similar to reaction formation. For example, a man may be frustrated by the actions of his boss and feel very angry toward him. His anger may make him feel uncomfortable because he is, in fact, dependent upon his boss' good opinion of him for his job security and for any promotion. He tries to suppress this reaction, he may lean over backward, as it were, in his relationships with his boss to be polite and cooperative. If he is conscious of doing this, then he is suppressing his feelings and acting in a way which he perceives as insurance against his boss' detecting his true feelings. If he is unaware of what he is doing, then he is using reaction formation to cope with his feelings.

We sometimes see people who are bound and determined that they are going to be helpful. Their behavior reaches such an exaggerated level that they persist in being "helpful" even when their "help" is harmful to the other person. In a stubborn, rigid manner they force their help on others and will not be satisfied until they feel they have been of help to others. Many times such helping behavior, if it can be called such, is determined almost wholly by the person's own needs and fears and is based upon reaction formation. When a desire to help is based primarily upon reaction formation, then it is usually unfruitful and may even be dangerous to others.

This point can be illustrated most clearly, perhaps, with a common example of a child's attempt to help. Johnny, who is four, has a baby sister who is one. Since the coming of his baby sister, Johnny has had mixed feelings about her. He did want a baby sister, and before she came he thought how nice it would be to have someone to play with. He found out, however, that she was not interested in the things he was interested in and that she was not able to do many of the activities that he wanted to do, such as play ball or go bug hunting. To make matters worse, she now received a great deal of his mother's attention, whereas formerly he had received most of his mother's attention. So there were some good reasons for not being overjoyed with having a baby sister; there were some good reasons, from his point of view, for being resentful and mad at her.

But Johnny had learned that he should not be mad at his baby sister. He had been made to feel ashamed and bad for feeling this way. Johnny was left in a tough position. He did have the feelings and reactions which, good or bad, were honest and sincere, but he also felt that he should not have them because he had learned they were bad. To have feelings that his mother viewed as bad really bothered him because he would lose her approval and perhaps her love. Consequently Johnny repressed feelings of anger and hostility toward his baby sister. More than this, he coped with them through reaction formation and became highly devoted to his baby sister, spending great lengths of time helping her to learn to walk. In this way he convinced himself that he really was good, that he did not have any bad feelings toward baby sister, and that he even wanted to help her.

The danger in Johnny's situation is that just because Johnny had deceived himself as to the complexity of his feelings, this did not mean the feelings were not present. They were still present and they found indirect, disguised expression in his helping behavior. Thus, in helping her to learn to walk, he would frequently "help" too much and she would fall down unnecessarily. He would also help her in inappropriate places, as on the stairs or on the cement floor in the basement. And he would give her "bear hugs" to show how much he liked her, but more often than not these were too hard and she would cry because of their pressure.

Whenever we are being overprotective of someone else, we can wonder whether this might not be due to reaction formation. Sometimes, of course, it will not be; but at other times it will be. When we are overprotective of persons, we are really not giving them the opportunity they need to learn new skills and competencies which will enable them to become more mature, independent and secure. Helping others to help themselves often requires us to cope with our own fears and anxieties in a way that will not prevent others from taking the next step forward. This step frequently is a calculated risk and not without some danger of error or mistake.

UNDOING

Through undoing we attempt to undo something we have done, or something we think we have done, and now disapprove of. We may try to undo or make up for an unkind word or act, or we may try to atone for thoughts or feelings that we have had which we experienced as unacceptable. Undoing is a way of coping with our guilt feelings and a way of regaining our self-esteem. It has considerable social usefulness in our society, and most children are consciously taught by their parents to make use of the mechanism of undoing. An apology is an act of undoing, as well as such behavior as giving another person a gift in replacement for something we have broken or giving our spouse a present after an argument. In all these situations we are attempting to undo, to make up for, something we have thought or said or done, and to atone for behavior that we feel guilty about.

We have also learned that by acts of undoing we sometimes can prevent punishment. The child that has done something wrong

frequently will betray himself through later actions of being unusually helpful to his mother. It is our recognition of this mechanism that has given rise to the common remark, "You must be
feeling guilty about something," that is often made when someone
is unusually good or kind or helpful. Such a comment should be
used sparingly, if at all, since it will not always, of course, be true
that the person is feeling guilty. Also, even though this were true,
it may only serve to make the individual feel even more guilty
and uncomfortable when he is already trying to cope with his
feelings about his previous behavior. There are many times, if we
really want to be helpful and are primarily concerned with another's growth and development, when we will not comment on
the basis of our understanding of what is probably occurring. It
is often best merely to accept acts of undoing from others graciously without comment, and let them rebuild their self-esteem.

Undoing, like other defense mechanisms, can reach exaggerated
and neurotic proportions so that it impedes rather than aids our
being helpful to others. This is especially true when we are unusually harsh in our judgment of ourselves, or when we have
repressed what it is that we feel guilty about. Then we may per-
sistently function in an undoing manner in futile attempts to
relieve our own guilt feelings, and be less able to be responsive
to the real needs and feelings of others.

There is the temptation, then, sometimes to feel impelled to
help others because of our own guilts and needs to atone. If we are
unaware of our tendencies in this direction, and we may be sure
that most of us are so tempted at times, then we again are in
danger of exploiting a helping relationship to meet our own
needs. The crucial factor, as noted before, is the extent to which
we can appropriately direct our own behavior so that it is truly
helpful.

EMOTIONAL INSULATION

Through emotional insulation the individual tries to shield himself from unpleasant feelings or the possibility of being hurt by
withdrawing emotionally. It is as if the individual were trying to
insulate himself from his feelings and the possibility of being hurt
by erecting a barrier. Such common remarks as, "I don't care. It
doesn't make any difference to me," and "I don't even dare hope" are
often examples of emotional insulation. It is as if we think we can

prevent ourselves from being hurt emotionally or rejected or frustrated by not becoming emotionally involved. If we remain "cool, calm, and collected" and do not let anything bother us or anyone get too close to us, then we cannot get hurt. Here the individual is usually just hurting himself because he is afraid someone else might hurt him; through emotional insulation he keeps others from hurting him through rejection or frustration, but he also denies to himself any gratification for his needs to love and be loved, to interact with others, and to feel that he belongs to the human race.

Extended use of emotional insulation as a way of coping with life's frustrations usually means that the individual will not attempt to develop his capacities to their potential. He will aspire to less and he will settle for less because he believes this course to be safer. He will be inclined to avoid competitive situations where he might have to face failure or losing; for him the thought of failure and loss of prestige is more painful than the act of not trying.

Every occupation or action has certain risks, and wanting to help others to help themselves is no exception. No matter how adequately we prepare, no matter how sure we are of the goals, no matter how realistic and objective we strive to become in our helping behavior, we too are human and we will feel frustrated, defeated, and hurt in our efforts from time to time. People in helping professions learn not to become overly involved in the problems of the individuals they strive to help. Just as surely, they all experience from time to time the humanness of becoming too involved, and of being hurt and frustrated. It would be a cold person, indeed, who never experienced such feelings, and it would cast doubt on his real capacity to help others. The risk involved in trying to help others is that we will be hurt at times; the remedy is our awareness of this risk and our capacity to let others help us work through such feelings when they do occur so that they do not endanger our relationship with the person we are trying to help. The real dangers in life are frequently not the risks, but rather the way we cope with the risks. To withdraw through emotional insulation will only result in our own diminished satisfaction and productivity in life and will help neither ourselves nor others.

To understand is not to be immune. Just as we can have knowledge of the laws of physics and still be affected by them, so also we can understand some of the principles of human behavior and still be affected by them. We will continue to experience anxiety, to squirm with our conflicts, and to fool ourselves. The hope of greater understanding is that perhaps we will suffer slightly less and become slightly more humane in our relations with others. With greater understanding we will also find that it is usually most helpful to say less and listen more; those who are most helpful usually find little necessity to force their understanding upon others in a verbal barrage of know-more-than-thou pronouncements.

Oversimplification is most dangerous when we are not aware of indulging in it. In this chapter and the preceding one some fundamental information about human behavior has been presented. The purpose of this book necessitated taking the calculated risk of oversimplifying and perhaps distorting a very complex topic. A little knowledge can be a dangerous thing, but it does not have to be; it can also be the stimulation to learn more. Just as it is true that all things cannot be learned in books, it is also true that many things can be learned from books. It is probably the better part of wisdom to learn from the mistakes of others rather than our own, although of course we will have our own direct learning experiences in this regard. We learn from our own experience by thinking and reflecting upon it. We learn from the experience of those we know by talking with them. Through books, however, we can learn from the experiences of many individuals whom we would never have the opportunity to know directly. Your local librarian will be able to help you locate sound, informative books about human behavior. Use this book as a beginning, not an end.

4

Readiness to Help: Eliminating the Negative

▶We really have no choice when it comes to helping others. We all engage in helping activities, at least to some extent. We also share another characteristic: we all must start with what we have, begin with what we are. In the tooling-up process of increasing our readiness to help others we must be willing to take an honest look at ourselves and assess our own strengths and weaknesses for effective helping. Our chief tool in helping others will be ourselves and the qualities that we bring to the helping relationship. Like all good workmen, we will be continually concerned that our tools are appropriate to the task. This will require a never-ending process of self-evaluation.

In this chapter we will discuss some common characteristics that are usually liabilities when we want to help others, and in the next chapter we will focus upon qualities that are usually assets. It must be emphasized again, however, that we are all human and that we will not eliminate all negative and unhelpful characteristics once and for all from our functioning. Indeed, some characteristics that might be liabilities when we are attempting to help others might very well be assets when we are attending to other pursuits. Our purpose should be to develop our self-awareness so that we may become more flexible in our functioning and better able to control and direct our behavior in a manner compatible with achieving our goals. Increasing our awareness of ourselves and increasing our perceptiveness of the reactions of others to ourselves are first steps in developing our capacities to use ourselves effectively in helping others.

PUNITIVE, JUDGMENTAL, AND REJECTING ATTITUDES

A person who functions in a punitive, judgmental, and rejecting manner toward others tends to view people as being "good" or "bad" and their behavior as either "right" or "wrong." People are seen as "worthy" or "unworthy" of receiving help and very often those individuals most in need of help are viewed as not worthy or ineligible for receiving help. More attention is given to determining whether people should be helped than to how they can be helped. The act of helping becomes a way of rewarding individuals for "good" behavior with the effect that those who need help the most are the least likely to receive it.

People who display punitive, judgmental, and rejecting attitudes toward others are usually unhappy individuals themselves. Their harshness toward others often reflects their own inability to accept themselves. They basically are rejecting not only toward one individual, but toward the whole human race. Unable to accept the realities of what it means to be human, they continually punish and reject people for being people. Their own functioning is governed largely by what Karen Horney, a noted psychoanalyst, has called "the tyranny of the should." Their primary concern becomes one of enforcing a standard, typically harsh and unrealistic, of what people "should be" by basically punitive methods.

The consistent display of punitive, judgmental, and rejecting attitudes toward others reflects a lack of faith in the capacity of people to help themselves. It represents a fundamental belief that people will be "bad" if left to their own devices. More often than not the very enjoyment of life is looked upon with suspicion and there is a tendency to equate suffering with being good.

Punitive, judgmental, and rejecting attitudes toward people were more common in the United States in the past than they are today. Both our religious teachings and our laws have been slowly shifting from what might be called a punishment orientation to a rehabilitation orientation. As we have learned more about man and his behavior, we have become interested in a person's past behavior more as a way of understanding his current difficulties than as a basis upon which to punish him for wrongdoing. We have become more concerned with determining how we can help people to change so that they will be able to lead personally satisfying and socially productive lives and less concerned with determining what punishment would be most appropriate for past wrongdoing. Our prison system, for example, is slowly reflecting the greater knowledge that has been obtained about human behavior during this century, with the consequence that it is less punitively oriented and more concerned with helping prisoners to become law-abiding citizens.

In efforts to help others to help themselves there is little or no place for punishment or for punishing attitudes. It is usually easier to punish than to help, just as it is usually easier to destroy and to criticize than it is to construct and to create. When we are punishing others, we are often merely giving vent to our own feelings with little consideration as to what would really be most effective in helping the other person to change. Punishment alone, with no learning experiences to help the individual adopt more acceptable or desirable patterns of behavior, usually serves to prevent the undesirable act only for here and now, and to foster smouldering resentments in the individual that will be expressed through the same or similar acts later on.

Just as individuals sometimes act in punishing ways because it is easier to give vent to feelings than to think constructively about what might be most helpful, so also do helping agencies and organizations sometimes adopt punishing policies for reasons of administrative expediency. It is usually administratively less difficult to expel an individual from the group than it is to retain him in the group and help him to become a productive member of the group. In our humanness it is sometimes tempting to do what is most comfortable for us rather than what is best for the individual we are trying to help, and then to rationalize our action as being for the best welfare of the individual.

Although for many organizations the successful functioning of the group is the important goal, this is seldom true in the case of helping organizations. The goals of Little League ball teams are, or should be, different from the goals of professional ball teams. Helping organizations usually come into being to meet the needs of certain individuals for help of some kind. Ironically, as the organization becomes accepted and moderately successful, it then often tends to exclude those individuals who were the original reason for establishing the group. Success for the group becomes more important than success for the individual, and those who need help most are least able to obtain it.

In a college dormitory, for example, the girl who is experiencing the most difficulty in adjusting to others often receives the most attention and support with respect to transferring to another dormitory, or to off-campus housing, or even to another college. The boy with delinquent tendencies who has the most difficulty in functioning within reasonable rules and regulations is usually the first to find himself outside the Scout troop or the Little League team, despite the fact that he might also be the boy who could benefit the most from being a member of the group. Helping others is not always easy: it is far easier to reject those who might need our help the most and expel them from our helping activities with the illusion that such punishment will be for their own good than it is to continue to work with them.

There is a difference between a punishing act and a punitive attitude. Punishing acts are *seldom* necessary when we are really interested in helping others; punishing and rejecting attitudes are *never* compatible with helping intentions. Because some events happen so fast, because some dangers are so great, and because some individuals do not have the capacity to cope with the event at the time, a specific punishing act may at times be necessary and helpful. An immediate spanking for the small child who runs out into the busy street is probably appropriate. Here a quick termination of such behavior is desired. Punishment is usually more effective when we want somebody to stop doing something than when we want them to start doing something. Punishment is usually justifiable only when we want someone to stop doing something very dangerous or very destructive immediately, and we cannot wait for the usually longer process of "accentuating the positive" to take effect. Any act of punishment should always be accompanied by constructive efforts to help the individual function in a more acceptable manner.

Punishing acts are sometimes confused with setting limits, especially by the person we are trying to help. Setting limits refers to the establishing of reasonable rules and regulations which are necessary for the well-being of the individual and others. The setting of limits in a clear and firm manner is especially important in helping individuals who are unable to assume complete responsibility for their own behavior. For example, the setting of limits is usually an important concern with children, with the mentally retarded, and with the mentally ill. The purpose of setting limits is not to punish individuals, but to help them order and regulate and control their own behavior in a manner acceptable to the world around them as well as conducive to their own growth and development. The existence of firm limits can be an important factor in a child's sense of security. Limits should never be set in a punitive manner, but only in a context of helping attitudes. Examples of reasonable limits for most preschool children would be not running into a busy street, not destroying the property of neighbors, not urinating on the sidewalk, and going to bed at a certain time.

Whether we are being judgmental, punishing, and rejecting is often revealed more by the tone of our voice and by our gestures and mannerisms than by our actual words and deeds. The words we say and the things we do take on much of their meaning by the way in which they are said and done. An act that is potentially helpful becomes even more so when it occurs in an attitudinal context of genuine concern and warmth; the same act can be harmful and destructive when accompanied by moralistically judgmental and punishing attitudes. The helping hand is often not enough unless it also reflects a genuinely helping person.

Think, for example, of the simple phrase, "Yes, I'll be glad to help." It can be said enthusiastically or reluctantly, it can convey real desire to help or it can convey a reluctant going along with the inevitable, and it can be followed by helping action or by defeating procrastination. Our attitude and mannerism in responding with this phrase can leave the person who asked for our help strengthened and reassured, or it can make him wish he had never asked us at all.

To make matters even more complicated, our attitudes and gestures are sometimes perceived in a distorted manner by others. How do we know when we are really being rejecting and punishing or when our intentions and actions are being distorted in this direction by the person we are trying to help? How much is ourself and how much is the other person? These are questions we will find ourselves struggling with as long as we take our helping relationships seriously. By being very honest with ourselves and very observant of the reactions of others toward us, we can obtain approximate answers to these questions.

If different people, in different situations, tend consistently to view us as a punishing, judgmental, and rejecting person, then we probably do lean in this direction. Maybe we will be able to do something about it and maybe we will not; perhaps we will even decide that we do not want to do anything about it. That is our choice, of course, but in order to be able to make this choice we must first be able to accept ourselves honestly as we are. We must be willing to accept the probability that several different people, at several different times, are correct in their perception of us when they see us consistently as functioning in a certain way. The scientific world calls this the process of consensual validation and for many questions it provides the best answer possible. It does not mean that the majority is always right, or that we have found the Truth this way; it does mean, however, that people tend to react to us rather consistently and view us as being a certain kind of person. This in itself is very important, since how helpful we will be with others depends, to some extent, upon how they perceive us. If people tend consistently to perceive us as being judgmental, punishing, and rejecting toward others, then our capacity to establish effective helping relationships will be seriously impaired.

OVERCRITICAL ATTITUDES AND UNREALISTIC EXPECTATIONS

Overcritical attitudes and unrealistic expectations for others may occur with punishing and judgmental attitudes, but perhaps more often they are associated with an eagerness for someone else to succeed and a lack of faith that they will be able to do so without prodding and pushing. Punishing and judgmental attitudes are usually expressed in moralistic concerns with the goodness or badness of others; overcritical attitudes are usually expressed in perfectionistic concerns with the competency and adequacy of others. Overcritical and perfectionistic attitudes toward others are seldom helpful and, more often than not, tend to increase feelings of inadequacy and worthlessness in the person we are trying to help.

Competency is very highly valued in our society, and most parents are very eager for their children to develop competencies that are held to be good. In their eagerness for their children to succeed, and in their anxiety lest their children not succeed, most parents tend to err by pushing too hard, too fast. Some do it in a narrow way, pushing their children to become "the best" in one or two areas, while others do it in a broad and diffuse manner, pushing their children to achieve in many areas. Whether the specific competency involved is baseball, dancing, mathematics, piano, or skill in relating to others, pushing Junior in an overcritical and perfectionistic manner seldom helps him to develop his potentialities to the highest degree. Even if we were to agree that it would be desirable for Junior to become "the best," and this goal in itself is highly questionable, an overcritical approach would be self-defeating more often than not.

There is a very real difference in wanting someone to do the best of which he is capable and wanting him to be "the best." Whether we are "the best" usually depends upon many factors other than our own perseverance and competency. It is highly influenced by the level of competency of those with whom we are competing.

When we are highly critical of the functioning of others, we never really give them a chance to succeed. No matter how well they do, we always comment on how much more they have to do or how they might have done it differently. The individual feels that no matter what he did, we would not be satisfied—we would react as if he were a failure. With this feeling it is very tempting for him to stop trying altogether.

Critical attitudes take many forms in expression. They may be direct and overt, with outright criticism of the individual's efforts, or they may be more subtle and insidious. For example, we may praise someone and then in the next breath undo the praise we have given. Most often we find ourselves adding a "but" to our first comment, as "That was a good job, Joe, but don't forget the next one will be tougher," or "That was pretty good, but I know you can do better," or "You really did fine this year, but next year the pressure will really be on." At other times we do not resist the impulse to make a comparison, as "Suzy, that's a beautiful gown. It reminds me of Sally's. You should have seen it. It was really something." Or, "That's a great piece of work, Jack. Did you know that Joe was working on a similar project?" Or, "Say, that's quite a string of fish. Reminds me of the time that I really latched on to them."

There is a time to let others know of the next task ahead, or of our own efforts or the efforts of others, but there is also a time to let others have their own "day in the sun," so to speak. It is true that nothing succeeds like success, yet how often are the success experiences of others quickly turned into experiences of defeat by thoughtless remarks. To say later, "but I was only trying to help," does not undo the harm that was done. The fact must be faced squarely, again and again, that our good intentions, important as they are, are not always enough.

OVERINVOLVEMENT

It is obvious that if we are going to help others, then we must become involved with others. It is sometimes not so obvious, however, that we can become too involved with others so that it interferes with our capacity to be of help. Unfortunately, we are often least aware of the extent of our involvement when we are overinvolved.

Some people are more sensitive than others and they find it difficult to help others without becoming highly emotionally involved. When we become too involved emotionally, our judgment is impaired and we lose our perspective on our own behavior, on the behavior of the person we are trying to help, and on the helping relationship itself. Harry Stack Sullivan, a pioneering psychiatrist, used the term "participant-observer" to refer to the kind of involvement that is usually most helpful. It is the capacity to be both a participant in what is going on and also an observer of what is taking place. At the same time we are functioning in what we hope is a helpful manner, we are also reflecting on our own behavior and the helping relationship. This is a quality that can be cultivated and fostered by everyone, but we do differ with respect to our capacity to become participant-observers.

The closer our emotional relationships with an individual, the more likely we are of becoming overinvolved when we want to help him. This does not mean that we should not strive to help those we are most close to—that would be ridiculous. It does mean, however, that we should be aware that we are much more likely to become overinvolved because we do care so much. The wise parent will sometimes recognize that, just because of his own overinvolvement and his role as parent, the school counselor or teacher or family physician may be able to help his child with certain problems more than he can.

In helping organizations it is usually best that fathers do not function in a helping role with their sons, or mothers with their daughters. Sometimes this is impossible, and at such times great care must be taken that the child is not responded to as a favorite or unduly penalized because of the danger of his being seen as a favorite. It is usually difficult for both parent and child when they find themselves in the same group as helper and helped. When this does occur, it usually helps if both parent and child are able to talk about the problems this situation poses, and develop some appreciation of the awkwardness of each other's role.

When we feel that someone else's problem is our problem, when we become more concerned and worried than the person we are trying to help, and when we are unable to turn our attention to our own problems, then we are probably overinvolved. When we are overinvolved we frequently tend to rationalize and overjustify many of our actions and decisions. We spend a disproportionate amount of time worrying about the problems of the person we are trying to help, and we tend to feel that he will not be able to cope with his problems without our particular help. We feel as if "the monkey is on our back," so to speak. With members of our own family we may become irritable and short-tempered. We find ourselves unable to discuss the problem in a rational manner with the one we want to help, and we are not able to listen sympathetically. We may find ourselves not even wanting to hear what the other person has to say because we are afraid we could not cope with it.

When we are overinvolved as a member of a helping organization, we may find ourselves wanting to contact the person we are trying to help outside the established setting or hours. Helping organizations usually have good reasons for setting certain hours or places where helping people meet with those who need help. The rules and regulations serve as a deterrent and partial protection against overinvolvement. When we find ourselves making excuses for transgressing the usual regulations in the name of helping, then we can usually be sure that we are overinvolved.

When we are overinvolved, we are no longer participant-observers. Our objectivity and judgment are impaired, and our actions are more apt to reflect our impulses than our thoughts. One of the best safeguards against becoming overinvolved is to have someone with whom you can discusss your helping behavior. This may be another colleague, a supervisor, a professional consultant, or even another member of your family. The important thing is that we have someone who can serve as a kind of sounding board for us and who can let us know when we seem to be in danger of becoming overinvolved. The very process of talking it over with someone else many times will enable us to curb our overinvolvement and function in a more objectively helpful manner. At other times it will seem best to withdraw and let another person who is less involved serve as the helping person.

OVERPROTECTION

Certainly there are times when it is helpful to do something for somebody else rather than help them to do it themselves. There are also times when it is necessary that we act in a protective manner toward others. Overprotection toward others is more a state of mind and a way of thinking and feeling about others than a specific act. It is a tendency to act toward others as if they did not have the capacity to achieve or to withstand stress. It reflects an attitude of "I don't think you can do it" which undermines the efforts of others to develop their own potentialities. Overprotecting attitudes never help others to become more realistic, self-confident, self-directing, self-actualizing, rejoiceful of life, and considerate toward others.

Overprotective behavior toward others is often rationalized on the basis that we are only trying to keep the individual from becoming hurt, physically or psychologically. This would seem to be a worthy goal at first thought, but unfortunately it will be found to be impossible when considered further. In the very act of trying to protect an individual from all pain and suffering we are crippling him emotionally and intellectually from developing his capacities to cope with pain and suffering. We are hurting him in a deep and vital way that will only render him more likely to experience needless suffering in years to come. To protect an individual from a small hurt today that will result only in his experiencing greater hurt tomorrow, when by experiencing the small hurt he could have prevented the greater hurt of tomorrow, cannot be considered truly helpful.

Some pain and suffering is an inevitable accompaniment to human growth and development, at least for now and in the forseeable future. It is a rare child who learns to walk alone without at least a few falls that are, in fact, painful at the time. The prevention of *needless* suffering and pain is a very worthy goal, but this must be viewed in a long-range perspective. If our lives are to be as pleasurable as possible, with the least suffering and pain, then many times we will undergo unpleasant experiences today to lessen the probability of even more unpleasant experiences tomorrow. On a physical level, for example, we tolerate the discomfort and sometimes even the pain of medical examinations and immunization shots because we believe that by so doing we will lessen the likelihood of our suffering in the long run.

On a psychological level, it has truly been said that nothing succeeds like success. However, we feel that we have succeeded, and are succeeding, only to the extent that we feel we could have failed, or can fail. To know the success of achievement without knowing the possibility of failure is a human impossibility. To protect an individual from the possibility of failure is also to protect him from the experiencing of success. Rather than overprotecting an individual in the futile wish to shield him from experiencing any failure, we would do better to turn our efforts to helping him to tolerate and cope with failure experiences. The fear of failure can be more distressing and damaging than the experience itself. It is our reaction to not succeeding, to losing, and to failing that is usually of crucial importance. There are actually few failure experiences that are totally and irrevocably defeating when viewed objectively in long-range perspective.

Overprotective attitudes can be particularly damaging when we are attempting to help individuals with handicaps. The person with a handicap often tends to over-generalize the effect of his handicap and to develop feelings of inadequacy and worthlessness as a person. Overprotective behavior toward him tends to increase his own devaluation of himself and to reinforce his belief that he is incapable and inadequate. Our goal in helping people with handicaps should be to help them minimize the effect of their handicap and make optimal use of the many other capacities they usually have. It is especially important that they be helped to see themselves as persons with a handicap rather than to feel themselves as being handicapped persons. The difference is not just one of words. A person with a handicap accepts a specific condition about himself, but he does not devalue himself as a person just because of his handicap. A handicapped person, on the other hand, tends to feel that he is totally inadequate as a person just because he is handicapped. The difference is similar to that between feeling poor and being financially broke; feeling poor is an attitude about oneself, whereas being financially broke is a statement about a specific condition.

OVERSIMPLIFICATION

Up to this point we have been concerned primarily with attitudes and ways of acting that are usually incompatible with effective helping behavior. Oversimplification is concerned with our beliefs and ways of thinking about people and situations. Oversimplification refers to making decisions and reaching conclusions in an impulsive manner without reasonable consideration of the issues and factors involved.

Seldom, if ever, would we be able, even if we had the time, to consider all the aspects of any situation or person. A reasonable degree of simplification is necessary and helpful; we can become overwhelmed by too much information and rendered unable to decide and to act because of our inability to organize all the information meaningfully. The problem becomes one of determining when we have given reasonable consideration to the complexity of the situation confronting us.

The unknown, the uncertain, and the unfamiliar are all conditions which are stressful and anxiety-producing for most people. We feel more comfortable and secure when we think we know the reasons or causes for events and happenings. Our tendency to seek the quickest explanation in order to alleviate our anxiety and insecurity leads us, more often than not, to oversimplify complex situations and issues. Our awareness of our tendency to oversimplify and our development of tolerance for not knowing and for uncertainty will be our greatest aids in avoiding oversimplification.

Several patterns of thinking have been identified as being both common and faulty. Three kinds of faulty and confused thinking that result in oversimplification are discussed here.

1. *All or None Thinking.* In our attempt to reduce the complexities that arise whenever we start thinking about people, we often group them into categories. Thus, we may group people according to nationality, or skin color, or hair color, or occupation, or any other characteristic. We then make statements about the category, such as "Yankees are thrifty," "Redheads have fiery tempers," and "Bankers are stern." Usually our statements about the general category are not wholly true. If we contacted all Yankees,

all redheads, and all bankers to see if the statements about them were true or not, we would probably find that they were true for some members of the group and not true for other members of the group. When we engage in all or none thinking, we make the error of assuming that all people in the group will have the characteristics that we attribute to the group in general. Even though most people in a category may display a certain characteristic, we will seldom find that all people do. For example, even though most mothers do love their children, a few mothers will be found who do not love their children.

All or none thinking usually results in what have been called stereotypes. Stereotypes are relatively simple, fixed beliefs held by members of one group about another group that are usually false. Stereotypes frequently represent projection and wishful thinking. The tendency to think in stereotypes is especially common in times of stress and conflict, as in wartime, when each group wants to believe that the members of the other group are "all bad" and they are "all good." All or none thinking is also found wherever there is prejudice. Actually prejudice means a pre-judgment. The prejudiced person pre-judges others before he ever meets them and acts as if all members of a group were exactly alike.

All or none thinking never increases our capacity to be of help to others. The greater our tendency to think in all or none patterns, the less likely we will be to relate to others on an individual basis and respond to their particular needs in a manner that will be most helpful. For example, if we are working with adolescents we will probably have read and heard a great deal about adolescents. Although we will have seen many general statements about adolescents as a group, we must remember that adolescents differ greatly among themselves. We will want to approach each individual adolescent with an openness and a willingness to accept him as a person in his own right, and not react to him solely on the basis of our general knowledge about adolescents as a group.

All or none thinking is usually an oversimplification of "most and some" thinking. In almost all cases where we make a statement implying that all members of a given group are such-and-such, we would be more accurate if we stated that some are or most are such-and-such.

2. *Anecdotal Thinking and Overgeneralization.* In all or none thinking we usually start at the group level and act as if all mem-

bers of the group were the same. In anecdotal thinking we start with an individual and then act as if all members of the group were like the one individual. In all or none thinking we naïvely accept general observations and apply them to individuals; in anecdotal thinking we naively overgeneralize from a few specific observations and experiences.

For example, we conclude on the basis of our experience with three redheads who had fiery tempers that all redheads have fiery tempers. Or we conclude on the basis of our experience at the dentist's when we were a youngster that all children will dislike going to the dentist. Although our own experiences and observations will help us to understand others, we must be cautious in extending our conclusions to all people and situations that seem similar. People are different and conditions change; our conclusions will not always apply to people and situations that, at first glance, appear similar. Some redheads do not show any temper, despite the fact that we may have known three redheads who did. And the dentist's office is, in reality, a less painful place today than in years past and there are many children who look forward to their dental appointments.

Many common proverbs and folksayings represent overgeneralizations from particular experiences. They are usually oversimplified half-truths that apply under some conditions but not under all conditions. Sometimes one proverb even contradicts another. For example, consider "Look before you leap," and "He who hesitates is lost."

3. *Causation and Correlation.* Every day we hear people make glib statements about what causes others to behave the way they do. Mr. Brown's fellow workers are quick to remark that his wife is the cause of his sullenness and irritability, Johnny's mother believes the cause of his poor grades in school is laziness, and the neighbors are convinced that Pete's delinquent behavior is caused by the fact that his mother works. People tend to be uncomfortable unless they believe they know what causes others to behave as they do. The fact that most human behavior is very complex and cannot be reduced to just one cause is very difficult for most people to accept.

This is not just true for our present generation, but can be seen throughout recorded history. The factors that are thought to be important causes change from time to time, but during all ages man has attempted to identify simple causes for human behavior.

In ancient Greece, for example, hysterical behavior in women was thought to be caused by a wandering womb. Other kinds of unusual behavior were believed to be caused by such things as tides and the movements of the heavenly bodies. A very widely accepted belief that persisted for many centuries, and is still believed to be true by some people today, held that strange or unusual behavior was caused by the individual being possessed by evil spirits or the devil. At a later date it became popular to attribute deviant and different behavior to the willfullness of the individual. It was felt that the individual purposefully caused himself to behave the way he did, and that he was "bad" if he behaved in a manner unacceptable to others.

Actually the concept of causation is a very complex topic that has occupied many of the best minds throughout the centuries. Today we know that the causes of human behavior are many and varied and still little understood. Fortunately, however, we can often be of help to others without understanding all the causes of their difficulties and behavior. For example, we do not really know what causes a person to be better able to cope with his problems after talking out loud to someone else about them, but we do know that this is often helpful to people with problems.

In helping others we must be very careful to avoid jumping to oversimplified conclusions regarding the causes of their difficulties. One error that is commonly made is to confuse causation with correlation. Two events are said to be highly correlated when they tend to occur together or when one always follows the other. For example, birds flying north in the United States and buds appearing on trees are highly correlated; that is, they tend to occur at the same time of the year. However, we would not say that one caused the other. Two events may be highly correlated, yet one need not necessarily be a cause of the other. The two events may occur together and both may be caused by a third factor, or they may occur together because one causes the other. The important point is that we cannot assume that one event causes another event just because they tend to occur together. Many misconceptions about human behavior can be traced to confused thinking about causation and correlation.

For example, it is frequently heard that overwork causes someone to have a mental breakdown. Hard work, by itself, has probably never caused anyone to have a severe mental disturbance. It is true that sometimes a person will become mentally disturbed after a period when he has been working very hard and putting in excessively long hours. But when we say that the overwork caused the mental disturbance, we are oversimplifying a complex chain of events and confusing correlation with causation. Often anxiety and conflict, about work or about something else, have resulted in the person's becoming less effective in his work so that he finds it necessary to put in longer hours to complete his work. Conflict, anxiety, and excessive worry may result both in overwork and in eventual serious mental disturbance. Because others can see the hard work and the long hours that are put in on the job and they cannot see the conflict and anxiety, they are more likely to jump to the wrong conclusion that the hard work caused the mental disturbance.

Any attempt to help others will usually involve some risk that we may be more harmful than helpful. To deny the possibility that we may increase another's burdens or cause him needless suffering is not only unrealistic, but it will also increase the likelihood of our doing so. Our responsibility as a helping person requires that we confront ourselves with the possible consequences of our intended actions and ask ourselves not only will they be helpful, but will they be harmful in any way. There will be times when we will be unable to help and when it will be best that we do nothing. Above all else, we must continually take every precaution that we do not add to another's problems and suffering through our own thoughtless actions.

Whether our words and our deeds will be more helpful than harmful will often be determined by the attitudes which accompany them. To the extent that we are punitive, judgmental and rejecting toward others; to the extent that we are overcritical toward others and hold unrealistic expectations for them; to the extent that we become overinvolved emotionally with others; to the extent that we overprotect others; and to the extent that we indulge in oversimplified thinking about others—in all these respects, we will be more likely to be of harm than of help.

5

Readiness to Help: Accentuating the Positive

▶What kind of a person makes the best helping person? Many kinds, almost as many different kinds as there are people who need help. There is no "one best kind of helper," just as there is no one best kind of teacher or one best kind of salesman. Helping others to help themselves is a process that involves a relationship between a helping person and one or more individuals who need help. We will find that no one person will be equally effective in creating helping relationships with all people. Some people will be more effective with the retarded, others with the gifted; some with the aging, others with the young; some with boys, some with girls; some with the shy, others with the outgoing; and so on. Just as those who need help are many and varied, so also are there many differences among those who can give effective help.

There are, however, certain qualities, attitudes, and approaches toward life that are found to an uncommon degree among people who are unusually capable of helping others to help themselves. In this chapter we will concern ourselves with ten of these attitudes. To the extent that we reflect these attitudes in our own functioning we will be able to help a greater variety of people in a wider range of situations. As emphasized earlier, the intangible attitudes and qualities that pervade our functioning and from which our specific acts emanate will determine our effectiveness in helping others more than any specific techniques that we may master. Helping relationships are created by helping people, not by helping techniques.

Two general observations deserve mention before proceeding to a discussion of specific characteristics. First, the most effective helping people are usually maturing people; they are people who, in their own lives, are still arriving, so to speak. Although they are generally seen as being more mature than others of their age level, they experience themselves as living, growing, developing people in a continual process of becoming. They both are and are becoming realistic, self-confident, self-directing, self-actualizing, rejoiceful of life, and considerate of others.

Second, the attitudes of helping people tend to be consistent and harmonious with respect to themselves and others. They do not exclude themselves from what Erich Fromm has called "the human condition," but rather view all people, including themselves, as being "more human than otherwise," as Harry Stack Sullivan would say. They not only are able to trust others, but they can also trust themselves; they are not only sensitive to the needs of others, they are also sensitive to their own needs; they not only have faith in others, they also have faith in themselves; and they not only can take a helping attitude toward others, they can also take a helping attitude toward themselves. Self-love and love of others, self-respect and respect of others, and self-confidence and confidence in others are not antagonistic and contradictory; on the contrary, they develop together or not at all.

DESIRE TO HELP

The deep feeling that we really want to help and the conscious intention to use ourselves in the most helpful manner possible are indispensable attributes of the helping person. Sincere intentions alone will not always make us effective, but without them our helping actions will be hollow mockeries. Effective helping relationships can never be created and sustained on insincere intentions and artificial techniques.

Sincerity involves basically a commitment to ourselves. In the words of Lowell, "Sincerity is impossible, unless it pervade the whole being, and the pretense of it saps the very foundation of character." When we have wholeheartedly and honestly committed ourselves to ourselves as wanting to help, then we do not have to worry about how we will let others know that we want to help. Bumbling and awkward though our efforts may be, other people will get the message. Just as surely, when our helping actions are not sincere, then we may be certain that the other person will sense this sooner or later.

There are times when just knowing that someone sincerely wants to help will be a help in itself. The sincere desire to help means that we do care what happens to someone else. This can sometimes be the essential psychological support that an individual needs to renew his efforts to help himself.

FAITH IN PEOPLE

Faith in people is a deep conviction that people do have inner resources which they can develop and use to cope with adversity and to resolve their problems. It is a belief in the capacity of others to be and to do. It is confidence that people, in their moments of truth, will find the strength to do what has to be done.

H. L. Mencken defined faith as "an illogical belief in the occurrence of the improbable." St. Augustine commented that "Faith is to believe what we do not see; and the reward of this faith is to see what we believe." Illogical and unrealistic though it may be to assume that faith will overcome everything, it would be even more irrational to ignore the impact of faith in the affairs of men. When the history of man is viewed in long perspective, the force of faith will be seen to have equalled, if not surpassed, that of reason. It has been faith more than reason that has led men to persist and to achieve the breakthroughs and upsets which have had the greatest effects upon mankind.

The very use of reason itself is an act of faith, and our reasoning processes in turn verify the impact and force of faith. Having faith in people is realistic because it does make a difference. Faith in ourselves and in others can often be the crucial factor that nudges the impossible to the improbable, and the improbable to the probable.

Faith in people strengthens our capacity to think honestly about ourselves and others. It is a false and shallow faith that leads us to ignore the realities in a situation and to avoid facing the inevitabilities of life. In the words of Tennyson, "There lives more faith in honest doubt, believe me, than in half the creeds." Faith, like courage, is not blind to rational assessment of probabilities, but rather enables us to ask questions and to seek answers in an uncertain and not always pleasant world.

CAPACITY FOR HONEST THINKING

The capacity for honest thinking refers to our ability "to level with ourselves" and "to call a spade a spade." It involves the continual struggle to avoid distortion and self-deception. It means being able to think about ourselves and others as we are, not just merely as our wishes would have us. It means being able to confront ourselves with the unpleasant as well as the pleasant.

The person who can think honestly is able to think in terms of probabilities rather than certainties. He makes an effort to distinguish between the improbable and the impossible. He attempts to anticipate the probable consequences of his actions, and he endeavors to base his helping behavior more upon rational decisions than impulsive conclusions.

The capacity for honest thinking helps us to confront others with unpleasant aspects of reality when this is needed. It provides us with the rational and logical foundations from which to speak and to act honestly with others when this is not pleasant or easy. Honest thinking helps us to differentiate between the act that is primarily a kindness to ourselves and the act that is a kindness to another. It is the kind of thinking that confronts us with our attempted rationalizations to avoid true acts of kindness because they might be temporarily unpopular or painful. The capacity to think honestly makes it less likely that we will become the fair-weather friend only.

Even in the best of helping relationships there will arise from time to time a conflict of interest between our own wants and wishes and the wants and wishes of the person we are trying to help. Ethical conflicts are unavoidable aspects of human relationships; they are dangerous chiefly to the extent that we try to deny their existence. The capacity for honest thinking is a necessity if we, as helping people, are to be aware of and effective in coping with conflicts of interest when they occur. Only through honest thinking can we confront ourselves in an impending conflict of interest with our commitment and responsibility to use ourselves in a manner that will be helpful to the other person.

COURAGE TO TRUST

Just as success tends to beget success, so also does trust tend to beget trust. The helping person must be an individual whom others can trust. Whether others will tend to trust us or not will be highly related to our capacity to trust ourselves and to trust others. When we have the courage to trust others, we will be creating the kind of relationships that will most enable them to trust us. If we are unable to trust others, then we will find that they will seldom trust us.

Nothing interferes with our capacity to trust others as much as our fear that they will hurt us in some way. When in our fear we withdraw into ourselves and nourish upon suspicion, then we foster in the other person a tendency to distrust us. We are then participating in what has been called a "self-fulfilling prophecy." We make the prophecy that people cannot be trusted and act to- toward them as if they cannot be trusted; they, in turn, then become distrustful of us and act as if we cannot be trusted. We then exclaim, "See, I told you so, people can't be trusted." To a degree far greater than we realize we usually find what we are looking for in this world. If we view the world as a hostile and frightening place and ourselves as inadequate and vulnerable, then we will tend to distrust others and to be distrusted in return, and the world will be, for us, a frightening place indeed.

A trusting attitude *toward* others does not mean that we will not engage in honest thinking *about others*. The situation is some- what similar to the situation that exists in the courts where a man is held to be innocent unless he is proven guilty. There is a very significant difference between inquiring and skeptical thinking by a basically trusting person and the same kind of thinking by a basically non-trusting person. It is the difference between the per- son who is basically *for* people and the person who is basically *against* people.

Effective helping relationships require that we be comfortably open with others in our sincere desire to be of help. As Carl Rogers has noted, the helping person must learn that "it is safe to be transparently real." The helping person must not be ashamed to be himself or fearful that he will be hurt, rejected, and ridiculed if he dares open himself to others. Unfortunately, many people are ashamed of their helping intentions, feeling that others will secretly or even openly ridicule them as being "do-gooders" or "suckers" if they admit to helping motives. Before we will be effective in helping others, we must have a comfortable acceptance of our helping intentions. If we cannot comfortably trust others to be aware that we do want to help them, then we are defeating ourselves and them before we start. More than that, we are insulting the people we want to help: we are insulting them by wanting them to participate in helping relationships which we feel are basically shameful.

SENSITIVITY

Sensitivity to others consists of a harmonious blending of the intellectual and the emotional, the rational and the intuitive, wherein we come to understand another so that he is no longer a stranger to us. Understanding itself is a complex term that has at least two usages and meanings. Sometimes it refers to intellectual knowledge about something or someone, while at other times it refers to a more intuitive and intangible feeling-tone that exists in a relationship. We may understand *about* another, and we may have an understanding attitude *toward* them. Sensitivity to others, as it is used here, refers more to an understanding about others than toward them.

Being sensitive to others is not altogether a conscious process, nor is it altogether an unconscious process. The person who is sensitive to others is perceptive of them as unique individuals. Both consciously and unconsciously he is receptive of minute cues, both in himself and emanating from the other person, which result in an experience of knowing of and about the other person.

The person who is sensitive to others tends to be more empathetic than sympathetic. Sympathy usually carries with it a tone of feeling sorry for someone, or even pity for them, that is not found in empathy. We usually feel sympathy for someone when we experience an uncomfortable and unpleasant feeling of what it would be like if we ourselves were in their place. Even though we are all more similar than different, we *are* different. Sympathy tends to ignore the differences between persons and to confuse similarity with sameness. The sympathetic person tends to confuse his own feelings with those of others and in the process often loses any sensitivity to others he might have had. The sensitive person accepts his similarities to others and goes beyond this, recognizing and accepting differences, subtle though they may be at times.

Empathy has been defined by Dymond, a psychologist who has spent many years studying human relationships, as "the imaginative transposing of oneself into the thinking, feeling, and acting of another and so structuring the world as he does." This is different from putting ourselves—with our values, past experiences, and so on—into someone else's place. It is the attempt to imagine how we would feel if we were them, not if we were we and in their place. People who are sensitive to others tend to be good empathizers, but not always good sympathizers.

Pity, whether toward ourselves or others, is a degrading and depressing response which never leaves us or others better off for having experienced it. Although it is very human to feel sorry for others, and for ourselves at times, it is seldom helpful. Feeling sorry and displaying pity toward others is strictly excess baggage when we are interested in helping others to help themselves.

The sensitive person tends to say the right thing at the right time and to be at the right place at the right time. The person lacking in sensitivity tends to be forever putting his foot in his mouth, so to speak, and coming around at the wrong time. Insensitive people tend to look without seeing and to listen without hearing. They tend to see what they want to see and to hear what they want to hear. They are aware of only that which is most obvious and usually most superficial. They are not able to read between the lines, as it were, and to tune in on another's wave length. Whereas the sensitive person is alert to the tendency of people to say one thing and mean another, the person lacking in sensitivity tends to take everything at face value and according to its literal meaning.

Sensitivity to others involves a sensitivity to ourselves. Individuals who are lacking in sensitivity to their own feelings and experiences, and who are highly defensive about their own functioning, are usually not very sensitive to others.

READINESS TO LEARN

The helping person finds people interesting. He wants to know why people behave as they do; he wants to know "what makes Sammy run" and "what makes Sally tick." Just as some people cannot seem to learn enough about baseball, and others about cars, the helping person is forever curious about people.

The helping person learns from many sources. He learns from himself by reflecting on his own experiences and being observant of his reactions and behavior. He learns from others by watching and listening, and by reflecting upon what he observes. He learns from others by talking and interacting with them, by sharing some of his own experiences and obtaining the reactions of others to them. He learns from those he attempts to help by being an attentive participant-observer. He learns from books and magazines, and from films and movies. For the person who is interested in learning about people, the world has much to offer and is seldom dull. The busy market, the crowded street, the playground, the campus, the secluded restaurant, and the shop or office all present opportunities for learning about people for the person who is ready to learn.

SENSE OF HUMOR

The term *humor* comes from a Latin word that means fluid or moisture. In ancient times it was used to refer to any juice or fluid of an animal or plant. Although today the term is used mainly to describe a mental quality or disposition, it is still used in medical science to refer to certain fluids. For example, the vitreous humour and the acqueous humour are transparent fluids in the eye.

Taking our cues from the ancient meaning of the term, we can think of a sense of humor as the juice of the mind that gives life its rich flavor. Life without humor is like meat without juice— it's tougher than it needs to be. A sense of humor serves as the lubricating fluid that helps to ease us through the tight and painful places in the ups and downs of life. A sense of humor serves to protect us from the friction created by taking ourselves too seriously.

A sense of humor, as it is used here, refers to a philosophical state of mind that allows us to accept the unavoidable twists and quirks of life. It is a capacity to stand back and view ourselves with an amused detachment, especially when we are in the process of becoming over-involved, over-serious, and over-impressed with our significance in the scheme of things. In the words of Thomas Carlyle, "True Humour . . . is not contempt, its essence is love;

it issues not in laughter, but in still smiles, which lie far deeper."

A sense of humor in its deeper and more significant meaning is not the same as a sense of humor as it is more commonly used to refer to the jokester and prankster. Most of what commonly passes for a sense of humor is really a perversion of a true sense of humor. The "humor" in most jokes and practical pranks is disguised hostility more than anything else. It is as if the mental juice of humor were diverted from its real purpose, that of helping us to accept and to tolerate the tragedies that occur naturally, and used to ease our hostile feelings past our conscience into expression. People noted for being genuinely and deeply concerned with helping their fellowman are seldom noted for being practical jokesters. Their sense of humor serves a greater cause than the expression of hostility or the embarrassment of others; it reflects humility more than hostility.

FLEXIBILITY

Flexibility is the capacity to put our sensitivity to others into action by being able to vary our own behavior. It is the capacity to act on the basis of our awareness that people are different, and that situations and circumstances do vary. Flexibility refers to our ability to function in a spontaneous and changing manner that is compatible with shifting conditions in a world that is not static.

Flexibility refers to our patterns of thinking as well as our ways of behaving and acting. Flexibility means being able to avoid the "foolish consistency (that) is the hobgoblin of little minds," to use Emerson's words. The flexible person tends to think in terms of alternatives; he is able to approach problems from different perspectives. The lack of flexibility is displayed in rigid, stereotyped thinking that remains consistently in the same rut, so to speak, regardless of whether it is productive of solutions or not.

We all tend to be creatures of habit and to persist in using patterns of thinking and acting that were helpful and productive in the past. As long as our way of approaching problems and coping with stress works for us and helps us to reach solutions, then we are usually reluctant to change. There are two realities, however, that tend to work against us. First, the world is continually changing so that approaches to problems that were effective yesterday are not always effective tomorrow; and second, there may be better ways of coping with the problem. Horses and handmowers can still be used to plow fields and cut grass, but most people find it more efficient to use tractors and powermowers.

Flexibility means being able to shift our approach when what we are doing is not working rather than just doing "more of the same." It is an attitude of "let's try a different approach" rather than "let's do more of the same." There is no one principle or formula or one set of a-b-c steps that we can master and forever rely upon to make us effective in helping others. An inflexible, rigid approach to people on the basis of preconceived notions will seldom be helpful.

Flexibility also means that we will be able to shift roles when this action is appropriate and act in a manner compatible with our role. For example, a man might be a father to his son at home, a coach to him at the ball park, and a teacher to him at Sunday School. In each role—as father, as coach, and as teacher—the man's responsibilities to his boy will be somewhat different and will require that he be flexible enough to vary his behavior appropriately. There are even situations that involve a rather complete reversal of roles. This frequently occurs over a period of time as children mature and parents age, or as students become teachers and teachers become students, with consequent changes in the pattern of helping relationships. It is not uncommon for elementary and high school teachers returning to college for refresher courses to find themselves to be students of professors who were formerly their pupils.

TOLERANCE FOR FRUSTRATION

We experience frustration when our progress toward a goal is blocked, thwarted, or impeded. The degree to which we will feel frustrated will depend, in part, upon the kind of goals that we set for ourselves. If we set very minimal goals, then we will seldom feel frustrated, but we will probably accomplish very little. If we set unrealistically high goals, then we will continually be frustrated, and in our discouragement we will probably also accomplish very little. When we set goals, however, that we can reasonably expect to attain, then we will usually experience only moderate frustration and be reasonably productive.

There is another aspect to the experience of frustration, however. How much we will be affected by frustration and the extent to which we react to it in neurotic ways that will impede our effectiveness and our enjoyment of life will depend upon our tolerance for frustration. Some people experience very minor frustrations as extremely upsetting, while other people are able to tolerate frequent and major frustrations with little discouragement.

There are some goals in life that we can achieve solely by our own efforts. There are other goals that require the participation and cooperation of others. The goal of wanting others to grow and develop toward maturity, responsibility, and the enjoyment of life is a goal that we cannot attain solely by our own efforts. The helping process is a collaborative endeavor, and whether this goal is obtained depends upon the person we are trying to help as much as upon ourselves. We cannot give someone else maturity or responsibility and we cannot make them enjoy life.

To the extent that we feel we are completely responsible for someone else's progress toward maturity and responsibility and the enjoyment of life, we will be unrealistic and we will find our helping activities frustrating indeed. We will also be a very poor helper, for we will have confused helping with taking over.

A more realistic goal, and one that we can and should hold ourselves accountable for achieving, is that of using ourselves in a way that is minimally harmful and maximally helpful to those we want to help. When we can look back over our behavior and conclude that we have functioned in a maximally helping way in our relationships with those we have been trying to help, then we can and should feel successful. When we are sincerely concerned with helping others, and when we look back and see places where we have not functioned in a maximally helpful manner, then we will feel frustrated.

Realistically, the art of helping others is a very complex and uncertain activity. The most effective helpers are usually able to reflect upon their activities and wonder whether they should not have done thus and so differently. We must be able to tolerate the frustration of not achieving our goal at times. Only when we can tolerate the frustration of seeing where we could have functioned more helpfully will we be able to develop and mature in our helping skills. Effective helpers are able to tolerate the frustration of being imperfect humans who are trying to achieve perfection in their helping activities.

We are also going to be human enough to care and to be hurt when factors beyond our control, whether they are in the control of the person we are trying to help or outside his control, interfere with his progress toward maturity. All students do not achieve passing grades, all boys do not hit home runs, all patients do not recover, and all delinquents do not become good citizens. And this is always frustrating when we have done our best and it has not been good enough. Real lives, unlike movies and fairy tales, do not always end happily despite our faith, hope, and efforts.

We live in a society that places great value on speed and on accomplishing things fast. In helping people develop and mature, however, progress seldom occurs at breakneck speed. Growing and maturing are processes that often cannot be rushed; even when they can be, it is frequently questionable whether they should be. Periods of apparent inactivity when nothing seems to be happening and when the person seems to have come to a standstill are characteristic and necessary phases of most developmental processes. Usually there is much more going on at such times than is visible to the eye; these are often "breathing spells" and periods of consolidation that provide the foundation for further growth and development.

The course of maturity, like the course of a river flowing to the sea, is seldom straightforward and direct. There are twists and turns, and even temporary reverses in direction, which tend to mislead the inattentive observer who lacks broad perspective and to frustrate the eager individual who wants to get there in a hurry. Just as each river tends to proceed at its own pace, sometimes slower and sometimes faster, so also each individual tends to develop at his own pace which also varies from time to time. Attempts to drastically change the pace or course of development usually require complex procedures carefully carried out by highly trained experts, and untrained persons should attempt them no more than they would attempt to divert the course of a major river without being an engineer.

The effective helping person develops a tolerance for frustration, but he does not experience so much frustration itself because of his having thought through the complexities of the helping process. His expectations for himself and others tend to be realistic and to admit some probability of achievement. He has learned both to be tolerant of unavoidable frustrations and to curb his own tendencies toward creating frustrations needlessly.

ACCEPTANCE OF ONE'S LIMITATIONS

Just as we all have some capacity to help others, we also have limitations on our capacity to be of help. The mature helping person is aware and accepting of the range of his effective helping capacities. Recognizing and accepting limitations as well as responsibilities is a hallmark of maturity. The person who is truly concerned with the welfare of those he is trying to help will not experience limitations as a threat to his self-esteem and personal adequacy.

There are at least two levels of limitations. One level consists of our being able to help, but not without help and consultation from someone else. At the same time we are helping others, we are also accepting help ourselves. For example, a teacher may be unsure of what to do about a shy, quiet child who tends to withdraw from active participation with her classmates on the playground and in the classroom. Or a dormitory counselor may be uncertain of what to do about an unusually noisy, boisterous girl who continually disturbs other girls in the dorm. These individuals may talk over their situation with a principal or dean, or school psychologist or counselor, or with a mental health specialist, and after consultation be able to cope with the situation in an effective helping manner themselves. It is very common for professional persons to receive help from consultants or supervisors with respect to individuals they are helping.

Effective helpers are usually people who are able to accept help themselves. The giving and receiving of help, the participation in helping relationships, are viewed by them as vital to the optimal growth and development of any human. They do not just tolerate help, or seek it passively, they are usually eager for good supervision and consultation which will help to safeguard the welfare of the individuals they are trying to help and which will increase their own effectiveness as helping people. The individual who cannot accept help himself, and who avoids relationships where he is in the position of the person needing and seeking help, is usually unable to relate to others in a truly helpful manner.

A second level of limitation consists of our recognition that we cannot or should not attempt to help, regardless of how much help we might have from others. There are several sources of limitations on this level. One limiting factor will be the extent of our knowledge and formal training. The person we want to help may need more expert or specialized help than we can give him with our background of knowledge and training. Except in rare circumstances, referral to a more highly trained person will be indicated at such times.

Another limiting factor will sometimes be the requirements of our role or position. Under different circumstances we might be able to help the person, but because of our responsibilities in our present position we may be able to help only to the extent of referring him to someone else. Whenever we have assumed certain responsibilities as a volunteer member of a helping organization or as an employee, then we have at the same time accepted certain limitations as to what we can do. Agency policies, for example, might determine the age level or the sex of those we can help. We will also be limited to the extent that we can help those eligible for our services. For example, it would be unfair to the rest of the boys for a youth group leader to devote too much time to any one boy; although he might be able to help the boy if he had more time, under the circumstances he might find it best to talk with the boy's parents about his need for more help rather than try to provide it himself.

Still another limiting factor might involve personal considerations. If we find ourselves honestly disliking someone and antagonistic toward him, then many times we will be most helpful by finding someone else to help him rather than attempting to help him ourselves. There are also times when, because of our past relationships with a certain person, it is best that we let someone else help rather than attempting to do so ourselves.

There is no yardstick that we use to measure our range of effective helping capacities. We must use our own judgment with respect to our limitations, as well as the judgments of others with whom we can discuss our capabilities. If we are in a position where there is a supervisor or consultant with whom we can talk over the situation, and we find ourselves backing off from discussing our helping efforts with him, then this may be an indication that we are going beyond our limitations. In some situations no such person will be available. Our own maturity and capacity for honest thinking and evaluation must guide us at such times. When we are in doubt about whether we are really helping or not, however, we can usually find someone with whom we can discuss the situation. If we have no resources through being members of a helping organization, then we can consult our pastor or physician. We are almost never so isolated but that we can find someone to turn to if we really want help.

6

The Art of Helping: Acceptance

▶The art of helping others to help themselves is basically the art of creating relationships with others wherein they are able to use us in a way that strengthens and fosters their own growth and development. The quality of the relationships we establish will depend highly upon our own attitudes toward ourselves and others. To the extent that we are primarily concerned with helping others to become realistic, self-confident, self-directing, self-actualizing, rejoiceful of life, and considerate of others, and to the extent that we have "eliminated the negative" and "accentuated the positive," then we will be accepting toward others.

AN ATTITUDE

Acceptance refers to our capacity to relate to others in a receptive manner with respect for their individual dignity and worth, and with faith in their capacity to grow and mature, to be and to become. Acceptance is an attitude of "unconditional positive regard" toward those we are trying to help, to use the words of Carl Rogers. It is expressed in "loving relationships," as Erich Fromm would say. It is a basic commitment to the right and responsibility of each individual to exercise maximum self-determination in his own life with due regard for the general welfare of others.

An accepting attitude on the part of the helper sets the climate, the atmosphere, for the helping relationship. It provides the freedom and security in the relationship which enables the other person to direct all his energies toward solving his own problem. When we are not accepting, then usually the other person finds himself, often out of necessity, using his energy to cope with us and to defend himself from our pressure. An accepting approach in our relationships with others is a necessity if our relationships with them are to be helpful rather than harmful.

The accepting person is able to let others be themselves, and in his helping relationships he is primarily concerned with fostering the other person's being and becoming. How accepting we are toward others is a test of our faith in ourselves and them. If we have little faith in the capacity of people to make decisions and choices that are for their own good, and to act in harmonious and considerate ways toward their fellow men, then we are going to find it hard to be accepting. We are going to be tempted, from our own lack of faith and from our own anxieties, to "take over" and to impose on the other person decisions that we feel are right and best. To the extent that we do this, we will be diminishing the other person's capacity for self-direction and self-determination; we will be undermining his confidence, his self-esteem, and his freedom to mature. We will usually be lessening our own anxieties and increasing our own security at the expense of the individual we are trying to help, regardless of how "right" our decisions might be.

If we want to help others to help themselves, then it is not enough to be right in our own thinking regarding their problems. How right we are will matter little if we are not able to present our own thinking in a way that the other person is able to use for his own good. To do this, we must first accept him as a person and not treat him as an object. We must be aware, we must be accepting, we must be nurturant of his separateness and integrity, of his capacity and responsibility for decision-making and responsibility-taking. We must accept that what is right for us is not always right for the other person, and we must recognize that the calculated risk involved is that the other person will at times make wrong decisions and act unwisely. Just as the possibility of success always involves the risk of failure, so also responsibility-

taking and decision-making involve the risk of making wrong decisions. There is no being and becoming without risk-taking, and
inherent in the nature of taking risks is that some of them will
not work out to our liking.

There will be times when, because of the specific nature of the
problem at hand, we will be rather certain of the correctness and
rightness of our decisions. This situation occurs most frequently,
and in most clear-cut manner, when the problem is rather limited
and of a technical nature. In such situations, especially, we must
remind ourselves of the words of the wise Dr. Zorba to the impulsive Dr. Ben Casey: "You know so much about medicine, but
so little about people." Our expertness will be accepted by the
person we are trying to help largely to the extent that we are
accepting of his right and responsibility to determine whether he
will make use of it.

There will be other situations, of course, where we will not be
on such firm ground. We must be humble enough, and strong
enough, to recognize and accept that there will be times when we
will not be right, and that there will be times when what is right
for us will not be right for the person we are trying to help. Certainly we have goals and values that we think are good, and if
we are honest, we probably think that some of these would be
good for everyone. There is nothing wrong with this, but we must
not confuse helping others to help themselves with imposing our
own values and goals on them. Helping and converting are not
synonymous.

SHARING, NOT MANIPULATING

We must also be continually alert to the fine line between sharing and manipulating. It is often helpful to share our thoughts
with the person we are trying to help, but this must be done in a
way that allows him to make his own decisions in light of the information we have shared with him. It is not helpful to burden
him with our persuasive powers and manipulations so that he has
to contend with these as well as his own problems. The accepting
person tends to inform more than manipulate, to share more than
persuade.

An attitude of acceptance toward others rests on a fundamental
belief and faith in the inherent processes of individual development
that will lead a person toward greater maturity when such proces-

ses are fostered and not hindered. The battle cry of youth as it strives toward maturity has always been some variation of the phrase, "get off my back." In a deeper sense, and usually without being consciously aware of it, youth are crying for the accepting attitude that reflects faith in their capacity to gain the hallowed status of maturity and adulthood.

Unfortunately, in our eagerness to be of help—and to relieve our own anxieties—we often force youth into passive compliance or rebellious spirit that lead them to make wrong decisions. Many of the mistakes of youth are made in an effort to prove that they have a mind of their own, that they can work out their own destiny, that they are individuals with integrity and dignity.

Take, for example, the situation where Susy becomes infatuated with Johnny. They are both sixteen and Susy has eyes only for Johnny. To her, he is Prince Charming; to her parents—well, they never do really see him either. Like the bull charging the red cape, they forge straight toward the target and bombard Susy with the error of her ways. Her parents err not in their concern, or in their thinking that Susy is too young to be considering marriage, but rather in their impulsive acting on the basis of their own fears and anxieties. Approaching Susy in anything except an accepting frame of mind, they talk *at* her instead of *with* her, setting their will against hers, berating her for her immaturity and insultingly suggesting that she is too young to have deep feelings and "to know the meaning of love." How presumptuous we can sometimes become in our blind eagerness to be of help! Moving forward in a punitive, judgmental, and rigid manner, totally convinced of their own rightness, they drive Susy into the position of defending her relationship with Johnny and giving it more permanence than she was probably ever intending. In order to protect her own maturing independence, her very integrity as a person, she feels forced to fight back and resist the onslaught. In such a manner are many of the foolish actions of adolescence taken; not because the teen-agers freely decide and choose and act, but because they feel driven to it by the pressure received from unaccepting adults.

What could Susy's parents (or school counselor or pastor) have done instead? They could have accepted the burden of understanding Susy and her relationship with Johnny, they could have attempted to "tune in" on Susy's wavelength and let her tell them about Johnny. They could have started where Susy was, rather than where they were, by accepting the reality of Susy's current relationship with Johnny and by accepting the meaningfulness of this relationship for her. In discussion *with* Susy, not by talking *at* her, they could have moved on to a consideration of various implications of the relationship and possible alternatives and consequences. Life has no certainties, but the odds would have been much better that with this kind of accepting approach Susy would have decided and acted about her relationship with Johnny in a way that was right and good for her.

THE CONCEPT OF SEPARATENESS

Acceptance does not mean that we always agree with the person we are trying to help, and it does not mean that we always condone his actions. It does mean that we accept the reality that he is a separate individual, apart from us, with feelings, thoughts, and experiences of his own. It means that we attempt to relate to another rather than to possess him. It means that we relate to him as an individual rather than manipulate him as an object. It means that we empathize and attempt to understand him and his behavior. It means being able to talk *with* him rather than *at* him, to converse in a dialogue rather than chant in a monologue. It means being at his side rather than on his back.

In my work with youth I have been continually impressed by their capacity to make wise decisions when given the opportunity to do so. We give youth the opportunity to make wise decisions not when we completely ignore them and leave them alone, but rather when we serve them as sounding boards upon which they can listen to themselves think aloud. In this kind of relationship they are usually eager to explore with us their thinking and feelings, their tentative decisions and potential actions. In a relationship with an accepting person they are usually more accepting themselves of suggestions and new ideas. Just as success begets success, and hostility begets hostility, so also acceptance begets acceptance.

Helping means making it easier for another; it does not mean taking over and doing it for him. Accepting means recognizing, and acting on our recognition, that the essence of being human is having problems, making choices, and participating in one's own destiny. Inner security and inner strength develop only as we gain confidence in our capacity to decide and to act in ways that help us to become the kind of person we want to become.

Acceptance implies a belief and faith in self-governing and self-controlling processes, whether on individual or group levels. It is reflected in such group procedures as student government in schools and colleges, patient government in mental hospitals, and democratic voting methods in national government. Acceptance supports and reflects the basic principle that individuals should participate in, have some voice in, have some role in decision-making processes the results of which will involve them. In religious terms, we must each participate in our own salvation.

Most of us are fortunate enough to have experienced a few friendships that are truly accepting. These are not the superficial social kind of friendships that are something like new shoes, always pinching and making one self-conscious. They are more like old shoes that fit comfortably, that let your foot be your foot and push out here and there; you are aware of the shoe, but it is a comfortable awareness. In such relationships there is a comfortable acceptance of each other's quirks and oddities. We may not always agree and we may not like everything about the other person, but we do like each other and are able to let each other be ourselves. These are the really helpful friendships that abound in give-and-take and just plain, honest being-yourself. These are the people to whom we usually turn for help in working through our problems, in accepting our trials and tribulations, and in celebrating our triumphs. They understand us, they like us, they let us be us. And we are usually better people for having such friends. They talk and converse with us, they tell us their ideas, they give us suggestions, they help us explore various aspects of a situation and problem, they may even get irritated with us at times in their own humanness—but, they always are accepting that we are not them, that we are we. It is this quality of relationship that characterizes the accepting attitude.

When we are accepting, we are essentially communicating to the other person something like the following. "You are you and I am me. We are similar in some ways and we are different in some ways. I like you, I am interested and concerned in you. I want you to make choices and take actions that are sound and good for you. I can respect your difference, even though I may not always agree with it. At times we will not see eye to eye, and at times I will get irritated because I am human too. But you be you, and help me to understand you."

When we are helping others in times of crisis, or when they

are anxious and worried with their own problems, then we cannot expect that they will be accepting toward us. The burden is on us for creating the accepting relationship, and we must go more than halfway in our genuine concern for the person we want to help. We must accept the other's irritableness, his anxiety, or his depression, and not become caught up in it. We must even accept his rejecting us and our offer of help. If there is a Rock of Gibraltar that provides support and strength in a helping relationship, it is the continual acceptance, honest and sincere, that emanates from the helper.

MAINTAINING OUR OWN INTEGRITY

We must avoid confusing being accepting with not being ourselves. An accepting attitude cannot be forced; it must flow genuinely and sincerely. In the context of a basic attitude of acceptance, however, we will sometimes have ideas and values that are different from those of the person we are trying to help. Acceptance has meaning only as long as it is sincerely rooted in our own integrity. Being accepting of others does not mean that we will forego our own values any more than it means that we will necessarily agree with the values of the other person. At times we may remain silent, while at other times we may openly express our own differing thoughts and opinions. It is how we express our differing beliefs and values that matters most. We can express our difference in an accepting way that respects the reality of the other person's values, rather than in a moralistically judgmental, overly critical, or depreciating way.

It is to be emphasized that our specific words will be heard and reacted to in the context of the total relationship we have established. At times very blunt, harsh words can be sustained by an accepting relationship, where as at other times the most accepting kind of words will be seen as critical and punitive, depending on the quality of the existing relationship.

There will also be times when we will have to confront the person we are trying to help with certain realities that he may not like that pertain to our responsibilities as a member of a helping organization. When we function as part of a helping organization, there will usually be limitations set on our functioning and there will usually be regulations of the agency or organization that both we and the person we are trying to help must abide by. There will also be limits that we will want to set in our own relationship with the other person. Setting limits is not incompatible with an accepting attitude. We do not live in a vacuum but rather in a complex world that is structured and ordered to a large degree. An attitude of acceptance toward others also carries the expectation that they will function according to rules and regulations established for the well-being of everyone. In accepting their separateness and their integrity as individuals we are in no way excepting them from the world in which they must live. We may accept and understand their dislike for certain limits and regulations, we may empathize with their feelings, but we cannot excuse them from behaving in socially appropriate ways in keeping with established laws and regulations. On the contrary, true acceptance carries with it the faith that they, like us, will find ways of living with both themselves and the world around them.

Acceptance, then, refers to an attitude, a pervasive quality, a way of relating to others that is as vital to the helping relationship as breathing is to life. It is honest liking and respecting and is not to be confused with tolerance, which implies "a putting up with someone." Acceptance of others develops as we mature and accept ourselves as "more human than otherwise." It comes from our own thoughtful reflections on our experiences and relationships, from our honest awareness of ourselves and others. An accepting attitude does not insure that we will always be helpful, but we can be sure that a nonaccepting attitude will practically guarantee that our helpfulness will be minimal.

The Art of Helping: Presence

▶The helping art of presence consists of merely being there, of being present without necessarily doing or saying anything. The art of presence can be considered the most important, the most simple, and the most difficult of the helping arts. It is important because it often conveys, more than anything else that we could do, that we do care and that the individual who is troubled, anxious, or upset is not alone. It is simple because it requires only our presence as a human being who is interested and who does care. Yet it can be difficult because it frequently demands an effective control over our own anxieties and fears, and a curbing of our impulse to do something active when there is nothing that we could do that would help.

In America we place a great deal of emphasis upon *doing* and *achieving* and being *active*. When we become frightened or anxious or feel helpless, we want to *do* something active about the situation. The stress of patient waiting, of being ready and prepared to act if need be, of standing by, of lending support to others by our calm presence, is difficult for most of us who have been raised in an action-oriented society. Our common query, "What can I do to help?" reflects the high value we place upon doing and acting. It is very difficult to accept that sometimes the most we can *do* is just to *be* there.

In our materialistic and achieving culture we tend to measure success by what a person has done. Too often we try to measure our own success in helping others by wondering what we did to help. We want to be able to point to a definite action or deed that we did, and to say, "that was what I did to help." With such a criterion of success, based upon our active doing, we often tend to feel we have failed if we did not do or say something specific. We underrate the importance of the helping art of presence because we have been conditioned and trained to over-value the art of active doing. To be truly helpful to others, we must develop an appreciation of the importance of merely being present and gain some perspective on why we have the urge to do something active.

We do not have to look far to find examples of the importance of someone being present. The two-year-old toddler playing in his backyard will make several trips into the house primarily to reassure himself that mother is there. He may come asking for a drink of water, or a cookie, or many times will just turn and leave again. The important thing is that the significant people in his life are where they are supposed to be. If they are not, if mother has left by the front door to visit a neighbor without telling the child, or if she is in a remote room, then the toddler usually becomes immediately anxious and many times may start to cry. Mother does not have to do anything or say anything—it is her mere presence that is important.

As the child grows older he seems to become less dependent upon the presence of others, but his lessened dependence is not as great as it often appears. We come to rely on and trust our past experiences and knowledge of the world to the extent that we do not have to have others immediately present so much. However, we do find reassurance from our knowledge of where others are or should be at different times of the day. Although they are not immediately present, we can check mentally and reassure ourselves where they are because of our knowledge of their general patterns of behavior without going and checking directly like the toddler does.

A CONTINUING NEED

As youths and adults we become more indirect in the ways in which we seek assurance from the presence of others. Just as the toddler comes asking for a drink of water, we also find socially acceptable reasons and justifications for seeking others out. We find a reason or an excuse to ask so-and-so to accompany us to a strange meeting or city, we rationalize phoning our wife or husband in the middle of the day, and we stroll over to the neighbor's yard on a lonely day to talk with him about a specific project. People need people although they cannot always tolerate the thought that they do. Even the hermit names the trees and animals, and the pilot names his plane. When we cannot find people, we create them from the objects around us and derive comfort from acting as if another human being were present.

Presence is a two-way street, however, and that is why it is a helping art rather than an automatic helping action. There are times when the presence of another can be more disturbing than comforting, when it can be more alarming than reassuring. There are times when we can help most by leaving others alone and by not being present. There are times when our presence can be embarrassing and inhibiting to others, and basically reflect an inconsiderate rather than a helping act.

We must continually be aware of the meaning that our presence will have to the person we are trying to help. How will he view our presence? How will he react to it? Will it be reassuring? comforting? motivating? Or will it be unproductively embarrassing? Will our presence convey faith and trust in the other person's capacity or will it convey that we don't really have faith in his capacity? Will it be supporting or undermining? These are questions that an enlightened helper must be aware of without becoming unduly hampered by them. Above all, is our decision to be present or not present based upon our concern for the other person, or is it based upon our own need to reassure ourselves and alleviate our own anxieties?

NONVERBAL COMMUNICATION

We not only tend to overemphasize doing and achieving, we also tend to overemphasize the use of language. The result is that oftentimes we, as helpers, tend to do most of the talking and most of the doing when usually it is more important that the person we are trying to help have greater opportunity for talking and doing himself. The art of presence involves our doing and saying very little; its effectiveness lies in what we convey through our presence alone. The act of being present or absent is one of the most fundamental forms of nonverbal communication, and even in our highly verbal society it is one of the chief means of granting or withholding approval.

Think, for a moment, of the question most often asked when there is mention of a meeting or social gathering or any kind of event that brings several people together. People are usually more interested in learning who was there—who was present or not present—than what was decided or what kind of activities or program prevailed. Judgments about the importance of a social function or group meeting are frequently made on the basis of who was present, and who was not present. Depending upon who was present, we tend to feel anxious and "left out" or reassured that we were not glossed over and rejected. Who was present at the latest committee meeting, the latest club meeting, the latest conference or council meeting are taken as sensitive indicators of status and prestige, and of group acceptance or rejection.

More than anything else, we look to presence as an indication of who is viewed as important by whom, and who views what as important. Although an oversimplified approach to a complex problem, information about who was present and who was not does carry implications about what people think is important. In a busy world where we can choose among the many conflicting demands on our time, the old adage that we will find time for the things that we consider important does have some relevancy and truth. The action of being present is usually taken as nonverbal evidence of our verbal assertions to the effect that we think something or someone is important.

As with all human behavior, the act of being present may be viewed by different individuals in different ways. It is always imperative to consider what our being present will mean to the person we are trying to help, and to recognize that there will be times when he will interpret it differently than we intended. With this caution in mind, several common meanings that are usually conveyed by our mere presence or absence will be examined.

AN INDICATION OF IMPORTANCE

First, and probably more generally true under a wide variety of specific conditions than any other meaning, the mere act of our being present will be taken by others to mean, "I think you are important." Of the many places we could have been, we have chosen to be present here. Regardless of the varied reasons why we might have decided to be present, they all indicate that we thought it was important to be present. The individual we are trying to help will consciously or unconsciously react to our presence as indicating that we do think he is important. Depending upon the specific circumstances, this may be reassuring and comforting or it may be frightening and threatening to the individual. Although we all want to be considered important, we are not all equally comfortable when we are seen as important.

We earlier discussed the importance of an individual receiving some kind of reward if learning is to take place. Rewards do not always have to be tangible things, and, in fact, one of the most powerful of all rewards is the feeling that we are regarded as important by others. When busy people who are viewed by us as having prestige take time to be present at functions and events where we are "front stage center," as it were, then we usually feel gratified and rewarded. We feel important, and our self-esteem and self-confidence are bolstered. Helping another to feel important is never a waste of time, yet strangely enough we often feel that we are "doing nothing to help" at the time.

The effectiveness of many special events, including recitals, fairs, plays, graduation exercises and award ceremonies, consists to a large degree of the presence of others. For each individual participating in the event there are certain significant people whose presence at the event will make it a success and whose absence will make it a disappointment. Although we can become too dependent upon the approval and presence of others, it is a rare person, child or adult, who does not feel at times strengthened and more important because of the presence of someone whom he views as significant in his life.

Although many of the most significant people in our lives are individuals we have known personally, it must not be overlooked that people whom we have not known, but only heard about, can play significant roles in our lives. This occurs many times because of the role or position that the individual holds. Thus, the presence of a chief executive whom we have never seen but have heard much about because of his importance in our agency or organization can convey a special honor to a ceremony or gathering. Attendance at special events, indeed, is a very important aspect of the responsibilities of any officer or leader. Although he does nothing other than attend, the act of being present in and of itself communicates something about the importance of the occasion.

Just as an important part of the work and responsibilities of a leader is to be present at certain special events, so also the responsibility of most individuals in helping relationships involves their being present at certain times and places. If a dormitory counselor is seldom present in her office or room, if a teacher who advises students is not present at scheduled times, if a leader of a boys' club or a den mother is not present at the appointed meeting time, then this is usually interpreted by others as an indication that the helping person does not really want to help, and that he does not consider those who need his help as important. In many helping relationships we make definite commitments to be present at certain specified times; when we violate these commitments and are not present, then we can usually be sure that others will question our desire to help.

Just as being present usually carries connotations that we think others are important, being absent when we are expected to be present usually carries connotations of rejecting others. Once certain helping relationships are assumed, then our behavior with respect to being present or absent is always meaningful to others and it is never viewed neutrally. The necessity of being present when we have committed ourselves to be present, or have led others to expect that we will be present, cannot be overemphasized.

There may be times, of course, when emergency situations arise or special events occur in our own lives that make it impossible or impractical for us to be present. In a civilization that offers as great a variety of communication media as ours, however, there is seldom any legitimate reason for not letting others know we will be absent when they are expecting us to be present. If we cannot be present when we should be, every effort should be made to discuss this personally with those involved before the time of the absence will occur. If an emergency arises, then every effort should be made to telephone or telegraph. When we just do not show up, without any previous explanation, then the person we are trying to help is usually correct in thinking that we really do not care.

Just as we let others know "I think you are important" by just being present, we can also let others know we think they are important by letting them be present. This is clearly seen in parent-child relationships when father occasionally takes Junior to the office or shop for a few hours, or on a hunting or fishing trip. It is also a sound reason for letting those we want to help participate in the planning and decision-making processes concerning activities and events that will involve them. Planning *with* those we want to help rather than *for* them often makes the difference between the success or failure of our efforts to help. This is especially important in working with adolescents and with elderly people where there is generally a hypersensitivity to paternalistic efforts to do *for* rather than *with*. When there is any possibility that those we are trying to help could make fruitful contributions to planning—and this is the case more often than we suspect—then it is insulting to leave them out of the planning process. Even when we cannot contribute much directly, we usually like to be included in the planning process. The psychological effect of implementing *our* plan or *our* decision is very different from the effect of being asked to participate in *their* plan. Excluding those we want to help from planning and decision-making committees tends to increase suspicion and distrust, whereas inviting representatives of those we are trying to help tends to increase relationships of trust and mutual respect.

"YOU ARE NOT ALONE"

Second, it is a basic characteristic of being human that we derive comfort from the presence of others, especially during times of actual or impending stress. Even when, objectively and realistically, the presence of someone else will make little difference in the situation, we find it easier to tolerate anxiety and stress when others are present. The mere presence of another human can be comforting and reassuring. Since recorded history the most extreme forms of punishment have always involved isolating an individual from others. Exile, ostracism, and solitary confinement have always been used as severe penalties.

The presence of another person when we are anxious or frightened helps us to control our anxiety and to function in a more rational manner. The other person serves as an external object for our attention and helps us to organize ourselves. We can release tension by talking to him. It frequently matters little what he says in response or whether he says anything. We are reassured by his just being there for us to talk to.

Under extreme stress we tend to regress and to become more childlike in many ways. Our fears give rise to wishes and hopes for someone who, like mother, will take care of our hurts and fears. Just as the small child is calmed by the touch of the parent's hand, we derive comfort from the presence of another. When others are not present, and we are left alone in the face of stress, we may turn to God and find strength and reassurance from our feeling that He is with us. If we cannot talk to others because they are not present, then we can talk to God through prayer. The experience of feeling completely alone, and that no one cares what happens to us, is one of the most painful experiences that a human being can have. In the effort to avoid the experience of complete aloneness, some people may even turn to a world of their own making which they people with others who do care and who are present, at least in fantasy.

The experience of losing someone we were close to, through death or moving away or whatever reason, is usually traumatic and anxiety-producing. At such times the presence of others can be extremely comforting if they do not overwhelm us with their own anxieties.

We tend to derive courage from the presence of others that we often do not have when we are alone. Sometimes this reflects our need for approval from those who are present, or fear of their disapproval, so that we walk the extra mile when we are bone-weary. At other times we derive security from knowing that things will not go too far or get out of hand because of someone else's presence. For example, children on a playground will feel safer because the teacher is there. The camper will feel comforted and braver because of his belief that the Scoutmaster will not let things get dangerously adventuresome. Our presence can at times be a potentially controlling influence that lets others feel more secure in trying their limits and seeing how far they can go.

It is as if we were saying through our presence that "You are not alone, I am here, I will be available if you need me." Our presence is like the presence of a nearby life raft that can be reached for if needed. More often than not we will not be needed in the sense that the person will actively reach for us. But if we were not present, then the person might not have attempted to help himself to the extent that he did because we were present. Knowing that someone will be present in a place where he can be reached if help is needed is many times the support that is necessary if the next step is to be taken.

"YOU ARE NOT FORGOTTEN"

This assurance is especially important for people who have had to leave their homes and families to seek treatment in a distant hospital or institution. Important as our presence may be during an acute crisis, it is equally important during long convalescent periods. These are typically periods when activity is limited and the patient tends to become bored and to brood on himself. A feeling of being forgotten can contribute to a relapse and can significantly slow recovery from an illness. The significance of gifts, such as flowers or cards, at such times lies largely in their being a symbol of remembrance when one cannot be physically present. What is actually said is usually not as important at such times as the fact of being present, or the indication of remembrance through a note or gift. The essential communication is to the effect that "You are not forgotten, you are not alone, you are still important to us."

In a similar manner, the presence of others that conveys "you are not forgotten" is the crucial element of many USO activities for servicemen and YMCA activities for civilians who find themselves on job assignments away from family and friends. These kinds of programs can be an important factor in maintaining high morale and often serve to prevent acute emotional disturbances.

Helping others is an art more than a science because there are no rules or formulas that will always tell us what the most helpful thing to do would be. We must frequently rely on our own sensitivity and awareness in deciding whether our presence would be helpful or not. The act of being present can sometimes communicate punishing and rejecting attitudes rather than supporting and helping attitudes. The presence of others always makes a difference, but it does not always help.

"I DON'T TRUST YOU"

A fourth meaning that is sometimes communicated by the act of being present says, in effect, "I know you'll be up to no good if I'm not here, so I'm going to keep my eye on you. I know you'll be bad if you get the chance." Even more than this, there is an "I dare you" challenge sometimes conveyed that tends to spur the individual into acting in undesirable and unacceptable ways.

Needless to say, this kind of accusing and challenging presence is not helpful and tends only to arouse anxiety, fear, and resentment in those we are trying to help.

Some limits, some rules and regulations, are usually necessary in most situations, and the majority of people are usually accepting of them when they are established on a reasonable basis for the good of the group. When limits are set with the assumption and attitude that others will abide by them, when we as helping people expect, and act as if we expect, that others will function responsibly, we are more likely to obtain responsible behavior from them. When, however, we act as if we expect others to act irresponsibly and hover over them with an accusing presence, then we will usually find irresponsible behavior. At such times, unfortunately, we often fail to recognize that it is our accusing presence and attitude of suspicion and distrust that is being reacted to rather than the limits or rules per se.

The teacher who becomes overly concerned that students will cheat on examinations and devises elaborate procedures of prevention, the recreation leader who devotes most of his time to insuring that property is not damaged or stolen, and the librarian who uses most of her energies to preserve books from misuse and theft seldom reflect genuine desires to be of help to others. On the other hand, the success of patient governments in mental hospitals and of student governments in schools and colleges is due in large part to the accepting attitude and expectation on the part of administrative and professional staff that patients and students can be trusted to make responsible decisions. The learning of responsible behavior must involve practice in assuming responsibility, and this learning proceeds best when it takes place in an atmosphere of trust and positive expectation on the part of helping personnel.

To a greater degree than we are usually aware of, or comfortable with, we are influenced by the expectations that others have toward us. If people consistently expect us to act in certain ways and show this by their own behavior toward us, then usually we will tend to develop and behave in these ways. We are more likely to be trusting and trustworthy when others expect us to be and act in trusting ways toward us. To the extent that we are consistently treated as if we could not be trusted, then we will be more likely to become resentful and think, "What's the use. I can't win anyway. If I'm going to get blamed for it, I might just as well do it."

The kind of presence that communicates "I don't trust you, I know you'll be bad if you get the chance," is seldom if ever helpful. The mother who is waiting at the door every time her daughter returns from a date may feel she is just showing motherly concern, but the daughter may come to view this as her mother's lack of confidence in her. After all, how can she show she is responsible and knows when to come in if her mother always assumes a premature initiative by flicking the light on and off?

"POOR LITTLE YOU . . ."

There is yet a fifth kind of presence that in a hovering way in muted form says, "Poor little you. I know you're good and that you're trying, but you just don't have the capacity yet. You still need me and I'll stay with you." In more blatant form it says, in effect, "You stupid jerk. You just don't have what it takes. You'll never be able to make the grade on your own." This is the hovering, overprotective presence of the helping person when his presence is not needed and serves only to increase dependency and feelings of inadequacy in those being helped. The muted form is perhaps even more damaging than the blatant form because it insults the individual without giving him anything to fight back against except himself. It usually leaves the individual feeling less confident and less adequate, with the vague feeling that he is somehow a burden and a disappointment to the helping person. He tends to depreciate himself and to develop feelings of worthlessness and guilt. He may feel vaguely angry, but is unable to express this feeling because the helping person is seen as "too nice." When the rejection is more direct, as in the blatant form, then at least the basic communication is clear and the person being helped knows why he feels disturbed.

There comes the time when Sally must cross the street alone, when Johnny rides several blocks away on his bicycle, when Mary goes out unchaperoned on a date, when Pete is on his own with the family car, when Alice goes for her first job interview, and when Jack makes his first call on a prospective customer alone. These are all red-letter days of success that depend primarily upon the absence of the helping person. The words, "You're on your own," with a withdrawal of the immediate presence of the helping person, can, at the appropriate time, be the most reassuring comment possible. It essentially conveys, "I think you are ready, I think you can do it, I trust you to do what has to be done, you are adequate, I do have confidence in you so be confident in yourself."

A TIME TO WITHDRAW

Certainly it is normal and healthy that we be somewhat concerned and anxious at these critical periods when the person we are trying to help first tries his wings alone. Mature helping requires, however, that we "sweat it out" at these critical periods and not undo the adequacy of earlier preparation by our anxious hovering presence. If earlier preparation has been adequate, then the best boost that can be given at such times is the lack of presence that says, "I think you are ready, I know you can do it, go to it."

A classic example of helping behavior that portrays vividly the conflict involved is that which occurs when we encounter a blind person about to cross a busy street. A direct, active approach that usually reflects little thinking and gives one an immediate positive glow is to take the blind person by the arm and lead him across the street. The immediate goal has been accomplished, we feel we have been helpful, and we go on our way. But in a deeper sense we have left the blind person essentially in the same place; true, he is across the street, but how many more streets must he cross? The helping process that emphasizes individual development toward greater independence and self-sufficiency requires that at times we be prepared to stand by and anxiously wait while someone takes a giant step forward. Helping others to help themselves is not just "doing good things for people"; it frequently demands a gut-level tolerance for taking the calculated risk and sweating it out while someone makes real progress on his own.

When a person is learning a new skill there may be times when he wants to practice alone. There are times when the presence of anyone can be distracting and inhibiting, and when privacy is needed for purposes of concentration. There are times when the individual may want to avoid the embarrassment he feels in having a significant person in his life view his bumbling efforts to achieve excellence and perfection. There are times when the desire to surprise someone with the actual accomplishment is of utmost importance, and part of the accomplishment is in being able to say, "See, I did it all by myself."

Not only must we be sensitive to the feelings of the person we are trying to help, we must also be sensitive to our own feelings and our capacity to control them. There are times of crisis, for example, when our presence would be helpful to someone, but only if we can control our fears and anxieties appropriately. If we cannot, our presence may well contribute to the discomfort the other person is experiencing. When a small child is hospitalized, the presence of the parents and especially the mother can be greatly reassuring and comforting. But only if the mother is able to control her own anxieties in the situation. A child already fearful of the strange hospital environment will derive little comfort from a mother who becomes hysterical and disturbed herself in the situation. At such times the presence of a more calm individual well-known to the child may be more helpful than the mother's presence.

In times of crisis, especially when a child is involved, the attention of adults tends to focus on the individual undergoing the direct stress. Thus, parents tend to focus their attention on the child who is sick, and a group leader tends to focus his attention on the child who is injured. In these situations we must remind ourselves, especially when other children are involved, that they too need our attention and presence. The hospitalization of one family member is not only a stress experience for that member, it is also stressful for other family members. Brothers and sisters of the hospitalized child, or friends of the injured child, may display regressive behavior at such times and are in need of special attention and reassurance.

When we find that our capacity to be present is stretched to the utmost, it helps to remember that the quality of our presence—the attitude we convey, the impact we make when we are there—is more important than the sheer quantity of our presence, the length of time we are there. Depending on the situation, there are times when a brief visit can be just as effective, and even more so, than a lengthy visit. The impact of someone's being there often derives significance from the knowledge that they are very busy, that there are many demands on their time, and that they did take the time to come. The length of time they were there was of less significance than the fact that they came at all. For example, the fact that a supervisor or administrator "stops by" can be quite meaningful regardless of the time he spends. The nurse who looks in the sickroom periodically, the physician who makes his rounds with a brief word for every patient, and the pastor who makes a brief home visit recognize the importance of their being present even if only briefly.

The helping art of presence, and its counterpart of absence, is one of the most powerful and influential techniques in the repertoire of helping behaviors. It communicates at a fundamental, nonverbal level our intentions, feelings, and attitudes toward others. It is an aspect of all our relationships with others and it is seldom without meaning. Our sincerity and honesty in wanting to help others, and our effectiveness in doing so, will in no way be conveyed more than in our sensitivity to the subtle and intricate language of presence.

8

The Art of Helping: Listening

▶We hear with our ears, but we listen with our entire being. A good listener strives to become as conscious and as aware as possible of all that is being said and communicated. He listens not only to words, but also to gestures. He gropes for an understanding of what the other person is trying to say, but is unable to say directly. He listens for what is not said as well as to what is said. The good listener is highly involved in an acceptant and empathic manner with the question, "What is this person really trying to tell me?"

Good listening is a searching for meaning. It is a very active and involved searching for meaning, with an attentiveness to the many and varied subtleties of human expression. What kind of a listener we will be depends on many things, but most of all it depends on our own motivation. We have to want to listen and we have to work at it.

Exactly how listening helps is still something of a mystery. However, most of us can verify from our own experience that there are times when a good listener can be very helpful. Somehow, after having talked with someone who listened to us in an accepting manner, we later felt strengthened and better able to cope with our problems. If we examine such experiences carefully, we are often surprised to find that the person did not give us any direct advice or do anything specifically for us. More often than not, we do not reflect on such experiences closely and we cling to the illusion that the person listening to us must have done or said something that directly helped to solve our problem.

A good listener helps not so much by giving advice or solving problems as by creating an interpersonal situation which allows the other person to function more freely and fully himself. Several aspects of this interpersonal situation which a good listener tries to create have already been discussed and need be mentioned only briefly at this point. Certainly the very act of being present and communicating, without saying a word, that we are not alone, we are not forgotten, and we are important is helpful and strengthening in itself. The accepting attitude that this person presents—noncritical, non-condemning, non-reproachful—further serves to enhance our self-esteem and to free our energies for productive rather than defensive use. In brief, we feel more comfortable, important, and respected with a good listener and, as a result, we are more able to use our capacities creatively.

TOLERANCE FOR EXPRESSION OF FEELING

A good listener can be helpful when we are bound up with our feelings and emotions to an extent that this interferes with our enjoyment of life and our productive use of our capacities. Most of us, from time to time, encounter such experiences and there is nothing abnormal about this. What really matters is how we cope with ourselves and our feelings at such times. Sometimes we are able to resolve our pent-up feelings ourselves, while at other times we cannot. Here is when, for many of us, although not for all of us, a good listener can be helpful. Someone who can listen acceptingly while we blow off steam, sound off, let our feelings out, even shout or cry, can provide the best help needed at certain times. A good listener at such times serves something like an escape valve; we are able to reduce the emotional pressure in a harmless way and regain our usual capacity for effective functioning by making use of such an escape valve.

This means, then, if we are going to be good listeners and let people relieve their feelings, that we are going to have to tolerate the expression of feeling. We are going to have to comprehend and understand what is going on, and not become judgmental or condemning when the person is making this use of us. For many people this is a difficult task, just to listen while someone else sounds off. The words used will not always, or even usually, be as proper as they would be at other times. The person may shout or cry. A good listener must be able to tolerate the language of emotion and feeling, which is quite different than the language of rational thought.

A good listener can also be helpful in another kind of situation, one where the person is in a rut with his thoughts, as it were, or in his approach to a problem. Usually there will be some emotions involved in this second kind of situation, however, and often progress toward solving a problem or reaching a decision is made only after there is some release of pent-up feelings. It is difficult to think clearly and to reach sound decisions when we are under the pressure of strong feelings. After the person has let off some steam, then a good listener can help him to think through his thoughts regarding the problem that confronts him. In this process the person is usually able to clarify his own thinking, put his problem in broader perspective, view it from different angles, and sometimes to arrive at a new and more realistic approach toward solving it. The listener in this case serves as a kind of sounding board.

Although usually a good listener functions to help someone express his thoughts and feelings, there are at least two exceptions to this. First, if the person is becoming hysterical or disorganized, a listener who is not a trained mental health specialist should help the person to regain control and composure. This can usually be accomplished by taking a more active role in the relationship, by directing and structuring the discussion toward a more specific and concrete level, or by refocusing the discussion on a different topic. When a person is unable to vent his feelings or discuss his problem without becoming unduly hysterical and disorganized, usually the help of a trained mental health specialist is needed.

A second situation wherein a good listener would often function to impede rather than to facilitate someone's talking arises when the person engages in an inappropriate confessional. The problem here is not so much the person's level of organization and control, but rather the content of what he is saying. How appropriate or inappropriate his remarks might be would depend primarily upon two factors: our specific position and our level of competency. There are times when, because of our position or our relationship with the person talking or with others, it would be better if he talked with someone else. Even if our position and relationships are such that this would present no problem, we must anticipate and make some judgment about our capacity to help the person cope with feelings of shame and guilt that might follow a confession of something deeply disturbing to him. Here, also, referral to a trained mental health specialist is usually indicated. At the very least, we would want to obtain consultation from someone who is a mental health specialist as to what should be done next.

IMPORTANCE OF LISTENING TO OURSELVES

If we want to be a good listener we first of all have to learn to listen to ourselves. We have to be sensitive to our own hopes and fears, to our own thoughts and emotions, so that we will not confuse these with those of the person we are listening to. We have to come prepared and ready to listen; if we are bound up with our own thoughts and feelings, if we are unaware of what is going on inside ourselves, then we will be less able to listen attentively and sensitively to the person we are trying to help. We must be sure our own receiving set is relatively clear of static and interference from itself if we are to tune in effectively to someone else's channel.

There is still another reason why our effectiveness in listening to ourselves will be a determiner of our effectiveness in listening to others. In a participant-observer manner, we will want to be aware of our feelings, thoughts, and reactions as the other person expresses himself. Many times we will find ourselves having reactions that will be sensitive indicators of what the other person is communicating, although perhaps not verbally. If we know ourselves and can be sure that we are not stimulating the reaction, then we can, and should, wonder whether our reaction is being aroused primarily by the other person. We can further wonder whether others might not be having the same reaction to this person, and whether this might not be part of his difficulties. For example, there are some people who tend to aggravate and alienate others not by what they say but by how they say it. The words they say may be fine, but their attitude or tone tends to irritate others and to carry more meaning than their words. If we are aware of ourselves and our own reactions as we listen, we can sometimes learn from our own reactions what we could not learn by just listening to the other person's words.

A good listener, then, must be aware of himself and he must be able to listen to himself as well as to others. He must be able to use his entire being, not just his ears, to listen to others and sensitively receive what they are expressing, consciously and unconsciously, verbally and otherwise. The better listeners we become, the more we will hear, and the greater will be our appreciation of the complexities of human expressiveness. We will find, in our search for meaning, that people frequently are communicating several meanings at the same time in various ways. This may not make helping others easier, but it will have a tendency to make us more reflective and less likely to make rash judgments.

We will have to be active and psychologically involved, then, to be good listeners. We will have to be alert and attentive to all that is going on in the relationship, and to the varied ways the other person may be trying to communicate with us. We will also want to be interactive as we listen. That is, we will want to let the other person know we are listening and trying to understand. Although there will be times when we will remain silent, there will be other times when we will want to let the person know we are with him, so to speak.

IMPORTANCE OF INTERACTION

Good listeners usually do not just sit like bumps on a log. They usually are able to interact with us in a way that helps us to clarify our own thinking and to express ourselves more adequately. They are able to talk with us in such a way that we are often barely conscious of them—so much do their words flow with our own thoughts. It is almost as if they were part of us and we were talking to ourselves and responding to ourselves. Good listeners are interactive in a way that facilitates rather than impedes the other person expressing himself, except in those special situations discussed earlier.

In becoming a good listener, as in most things, the opportunity to practice and to obtain feedback on how we are doing is important and helpful. We tend to take listening so much for granted that most of us are relatively unaware of what we are doing when we are listening. If at all possible, obtain a tape recorder and listen to yourself after you have been listening to someone. You can practice this with a friend, and each can take turns being the helpful listener. If you have children, let your friend pretend that she is a child or adolescent coming to talk over a problem with mother or father, as the case may be. Be sure, however, that you both know the practice session is being taped; tape recorders should never be used without everyone present giving consent to their use. If it is not possible to find a tape recorder, then sometimes you can find a third person who will function as a tape recorder and tell you what you said and how you acted.

Be prepared for a surprise if you try this. Almost everyone has habits, mannerisms, and patterns of speech and action that they are unaware of. These are sometimes annoying or distracting to others. Remember again, we are all more human than otherwise. Listen to yourself as a friend, not as a critic. After all, if you cannot help yourself, how are you going to help others? Acceptance toward ourselves is as needed as acceptance toward others. With a little patience, a little kindness, lots of motivation and some practice you will find that you can become a better listener.

When we are self-consciously striving to be a better listener and to help others express themselves, we often ask too many direct questions. If we feel awkward, our questions will probably sound awkward too. Without realizing it, we can sometimes sound like we are putting someone through the third degree with our questions. Too many direct questions sometimes have a way of sounding like accusations.

If you tend to use too many questions, try making comments instead. The exact words are usually unimportant and will vary from person to person and situation to situation. Be yourself. Let your interest and sincerity show. Try and express your understanding, if you do understand, and let the other person know you are with him. Comments like, "I see," "I see what you mean," and even "uh-huh" can reflect your concern and interest. When you are not really sure what the person is saying, say so. For example, "I think I may have lost you. Is this what you're saying? —————," or "I'm not sure I got that. Did you mean to say —————." The important point is that good listeners are able to reflect to the person talking their understanding, or are able to express their possible misunderstanding as it occurs. They are concerned, they are involved, and they are not afraid to let their genuine concern and interest be expressed.

Think back to a situation where you felt someone was a good

listener to you. What went on? How did this listener behave and respond? Why do you think he was a good listener? Our greatest clues in becoming more effective helpers are often obtained as we reflect on experiences when we felt we were helped. Usually we will find that people we consider good listeners were able to give us some feedback; they interacted with us as we talked without getting in our way. They expressed their concern and interest, helped us to clarify our own thoughts, and in return we felt supported, encouraged, and more secure. Their interaction and comments helped us to feel free to talk.

BEYOND WORDS

When we are listening, then, we will want to listen to many levels of expression and for many levels of meaning. We will, of course, be concerned with the literal meaning of what the person is saying. We will be listening as accurately as possible to the words themselves, and will want to understand clearly what the words mean to the person who is using them, not just ourselves. Sometimes the same word may mean different things to different people.

It is oftentimes helpful to repeat what the person is saying so that we can be sure we have the meaning he is trying to convey. This many times helps to prevent simple distortions that are easily made. In times of crisis, especially, when a person is upset and disturbed, he will frequently not be as clear and precise as he would be at other times. He may literally say words that he does not mean. This becomes particularly important when the person is trying to give information about what kind of help is needed and where. For example, it sometimes happens that a person phones for help when a sudden calamity of some kind has occurred, such as an accident, and asks for quick help but forgets to give the address where help is to be sent.

In helping relationships, especially with groups in an organization, it is frequently necessary that definite arrangements be made for time and place of meetings. The best of intentions can easily go to naught if the helping person fails to listen attentively himself, and fails to make sure all group members have heard and understood the conclusions reached by the group.

When someone is upset and is attempting to tell us something in a confused and disorganized manner, it is not only helpful for our greater understanding, but it is also helpful for the other person when we calmly, but firmly, slow him down and ask him to be more specific and precise. This serves to help him regain control of himself as he becomes more focused, in our firm but gentle presence, on what he wants to say.

A good starting place, then, is to be sure of what the other person is saying on a literal level. Here we must not be afraid to expose our own ignorance; we must be able, in a humble and direct manner, to seek and ask for clarification. We must be continually alert that we not assume that we know what the person is saying and gloss over important aspects. We must also be careful not to react with irritation to the other person's confusion; to do so usually results in an even greater inability by the other person to express himself.

At the other extreme, we must also be careful not to become rigidly blinded by the literal meaning of what someone is saying. We must also learn to listen "in context"; we must not become so rigidly attuned to individual words that we lose sight of the background and larger context in which they occur. Emotional and interpersonal meanings, especially, are often conveyed in the larger context and not by the literal meaning of words.

A few examples will help to clarify. Susy is four and it is bedtime. The questions now begin to flow more than ever as every parent knows. The more mother responds, the more Susy asks. "Mommy, can I have a drink of water? What are elephants good for? My toe itches, will you scratch it?" Only in the greater context of the hour of the day and the activity at hand do these questions yield their true meaning and significance. Susy is testing the limits with Mommy, and Mommy soon stops responding to the literal meaning of the words and responds to their deeper meaning, perhaps commenting, "I know you don't want to go to sleep now, but it's bedtime."

A youth stands on the train platform with his parents and sweetheart. His luggage and books convey that he is probably heading back to college after a brief visit home. Father and son talk about the weather. As the train whistle sounds, father shakes the youth's hand and the youth feels the pressure of money in his palm. He smiles, clasps his father's arm with his free hand, and says, "Thanks, Dad, for everything." Love and concern, the desire to be needed and to be of help, are expressed in many ways and not always by words.

Twelve-year-old Sally runs into the classroom noisily shouting, "I hate that Johnny." The teacher smiles, knowing full well that Sally will be anxiously seeking out Johnny as soon as class is dismissed.

A widower lives at the local YMCA and spends most of his evenings reading the paper in the lobby. Although there is a large clock at one end of the lobby, the widower usually strolls over to the desk clerk once or twice each evening to ask the time and to adjust his watch. The desk clerk tells him the time and never mentions the large clock on the wall. Loneliness is seldom expressed directly in so many words, but more often by actions.

In all these situations the meaning of what is said is obtained from the context in which it occurs. The good listener must not become blinded by the literal meaning of words; he must listen beyond these to obtain their true significance. As Theodor Reik, a noted psychoanalyst, has stated, he must listen with his "third ear." Helpful listening goes beyond the surface; it is sensitive to the currents of meaning that never break the verbal surface.

At no time will our listening be more important than when someone is calling for help, and at no time will we have to listen so much with our "third ear" if we are to become adept at receiving this call in its varied expressions. There will be times when the call for help will sound loud and clear, but more often it will come as a muted whisper that frequently goes unheard. There will even be times when the literal denial of need for help will be a means of its expression. Only our sensitivity to deeper feelings and to situational and interpersonal contexts will help us to detect when the call for help is really being sounded.

READINESS TO ACCEPT HELP

People vary widely in their readiness to seek and accept help from others, and this is true even when they recognize they need help and could benefit from help. Effectiveness in helping others requires that we not only listen for the call for help, in all its varied forms, but that we also listen for its deeper meaning as it relates to the person's readiness to accept help. In all helping situations we must start where the person is that we want to help. That is, we cannot be several steps behind or several steps ahead of him and be effective. We must learn to recognize when someone is seeking help, and we must also learn to tune in on his readiness to accept help. To ask for help and to be ready to use help are two different matters. We often must first help the person to become accepting of the reality and limitations of the helping process before he will be able to make effective use of help. To summarize briefly, we must be able to hear the call for help in all its varied forms, and we must be able to ascertain what it means to the person.

Two examples may help clarify the foregoing. Johnny has been apprehended for stealing a car, and the judge has instructed Johnny to visit the probation officer for an hour each week. Johnny vigorously protested that he didn't need that kind of help, he was "just joyriding" and really didn't intend to keep the car. During his first session with the probation officer he kept protesting that he didn't want or need any special help. Despite his protests, however, he did talk a great deal about his life at home and how unfair he thought his parents were. His protests were like "last ditch stands" and were his way of saving face; the more he felt the need for help and someone to talk to, the louder he proclaimed his lack of need for help. Johnny couldn't ask for help directly and verbally, but he could make use of a relationship with a helping person.

Paul, another boy in the same situation, quickly admitted he was "all fouled up" and needed help. However, he tended to pose his problem as he saw it, over and over in a direct and simple manner, and then to sit back as if waiting for the probation officer to solve it for him. Paul was able to ask for help directly, but he was unable to make effective use of it. Only as he gradually came to see and accept that the probation officer had no magic wand to change his life circumstances and that he, himself, would have to work at it was he able to do something constructive about his situation and his manner of coping with it.

The same situation is commonly seen in pupils' approaches to teachers and parents for help with their homework. One child will state vehemently that he doesn't need any help, but then will go right ahead and make effective use of help from parent or teacher. Another child will openly ask for help, but will expect the parent to do it for him. An important part of many helping procedures involves helping the individual to achieve more harmony between his behavior and his verbal statements regarding needing and accepting help. We are usually most able to use help effectively when we are not in conflict about seeking and using it, and when we are accepting of our own responsibilities in the helping process. When our sensitivity and our "third ear" tell us that the individual is in conflict about his need for help and readiness to make use of help, then often we can help him most by helping him to become comfortable with his need for help.

SIGNIFICANCE OF BEHAVIOR CHANGES

We must learn to listen carefully, then, to the literal meaning of the words that are expressed but at the same time listen for the broader and often more significant meanings that are conveyed by the situational and psychological context in which the words are spoken. We must be attentive to what is expressed in the relationship on a nonverbal level through actions, gestures, and mannerisms. We must also learn to listen for what is not said, because in some situations this will be even more meaningful than what is said directly. When an individual has been disappointed by something, when he has not achieved a hoped for goal, he may suddenly stop talking about it even though he may still be hurting inside. Or an individual may avoid talking about something because he feels guilty about it.

Again, some everyday examples may be helpful. When Sally has been talking for weeks about the prom and about Joe, and then suddenly stops talking about either and acting withdrawn and irritable, the answer is usually apparent to her friends and family. When Jack is unusually silent on report card day, this is usually communicative to his parents.

Whenever there are distinct shifts and changes in a person's behavior, verbal or otherwise, we need all the sensitivity of our "third ear." We have to listen "in context" and be aware of what is not said as well as what is said. Sometimes, however, we may be faced with an overflow of words rather than by silent withdrawal. It is not uncommon for some people to talk rapidly about almost anything except that which is bothering them most in an attempt to ward off their anxiety, guilt, or fear.

The art of listening requires that we be aware of what is going on in broad perspective and that we be able to consider more than one possibility of what is involved before acting or speaking. There will be times when it will be most helpful to flow with the person and to let him talk about what he will or remain silent, while at other times it will be a kindness to comment directly on what we believe is troubling him. These are not always easy judgments to make, but responsible helping behavior demands that we first be aware and accept the choice that confronts us, and then act in a manner we can live with.

There are times when we just have to gulp and say, in effect, "I know something is troubling you, but I don't know what. If it would help to tell me, I'll be glad to listen. Or maybe you'd like to talk to someone else about it. That's OK too." The capacity to say words to this effect is becoming more and more important in a world that is becoming more and more depersonalized. It is not enough to tell ourselves that we do care what happens to people and then to stand idly by at times when all our senses tell us someone is in trouble. More often than not, when someone is showing by his changed behavior (whether more silent or more talkative, active or withdrawn) that something is troubling him, he is also indirectly asking for help. The risk of being rebuffed, of looking like a jerk, of having to eat humble pie, should not stop us from making some gesture of helpfulness. Except in unusual circumstances help should not be forced on others, but neither should it be actively witheld because of our own fear of being wrong. We must have faith in our own sensitivity to another's need for help, and when we feel the time is ripe and somebody is letting us know he is troubled, take the calculated risk of offering our help.

DANGER OF DISTORTION

If we are going to be responsible listeners we must also be continually alert to our tendencies to distort, misperceive and misinterpret what we hear. We can be sure that, at one time or another, we will fall prey to our own humanness in this regard. Our greatest protection, again, will be our capacity for reflective self-awareness. Only as we are sensitive to ourselves will we be able to check and control our tendencies toward distortion and misinterpretation of what the other person is saying.

Our feelings and emotions can sometimes interfere with our effective listening. Our fears and anxieties may give rise to our not hearing what is said. That is, we will miss the point and not hear what the other person is saying because we really do not want to hear it; to hear it would only make us anxious and fearful. This can happen on a conscious level or it can happen unconsciously.

Our sensitivity to the other person is diminished by the interference of our rising anxiety. Common examples of this are often seen when adolescents raise questions regarding sexual behavior or elderly people start to talk of death. At such times the middle-aged adult usually becomes uneasy and anxious, and he may act as if the topic never came up. In his effort to maintain his own comfort, he may quickly brush the topic aside with a curt remark or he may distort its real significance and respond on a superficial level.

At the other extreme, our hopes and wishes can sometimes lead us to hear more than is being said. Actually we are maintaining our own comfort and security at such times by hearing what we want to hear. Although usually this will take the form of distorting what the other person is saying in the direction of good news, sometimes the distortion is in the direction of bad news. For example, a helping person with strong needs for others to be dependent on him may hear others asking for help when such is actually not the case. Only as we are aware of our internal pushes and pulls, our wishes and fears, will we be able to curb our tendency to distort and misinterpret what we hear.

The nature of the knowledge and information we have about the person we are trying to help can also contribute at times to misinterpretation and distortion of what the person is saying. When our information is faulty and inaccurate, of course, we will find ourselves in difficulty. Misinformation can be more harmful than lack of information, especially if we are unaware of the fact that we are misinformed. Tendencies toward oversimplified thinking based on stereotypes and popular myths about people are especially dangerous.

Even when our information is accurate, however, it can sometimes interfere with our effective listening if we are not careful. Both too little and too much information can be equally disastrous. A Scout leader, for example, that did not know a Scout's father had recently died would probably be less responsive to the boy's questions and comments regarding father and death. If a youth leader did not know that a particular youth had experienced a frightening night in a destructive tornado, he might be puzzled and unresponsive to the boy's anxious comments about a rising wind while on a hike. We can often be more responsive and helpful when we are aware of particular incidents in an individual's life; we will listen differently, and more meaningfully, on the basis of our knowledge about the person.

It is also usually helpful to know something about the general conditions under which the person lives, especially if these are quite different from those we are used to. Two children, for example, may make the same comment upon entering a cabin where they will be living at summer camp, but the comment might have very different meanings depending upon their background of experience. One child, with the comment, "Gosh, look at the bunks. Are we really going to live here?" may be saying, in effect, "This is great. Look at all the space," if he comes from a very crowded home situation where several people sleep in the same room and he shares a bed with other children. Another child, with the same comment, may be saying, "This is lousy. Look at how crowded it is," if he has been used to having his own private room.

Accurate background information about specific unusual incidents, about general home and social conditions, and about different customs and practices can often help us to be more sensitive and responsive listeners. Sometimes, however, the opposite is true. Sometimes we can have so much information that we become confused by it all, and we use more energy in trying to remember what we were told or read than we do in relating to the person we are trying to help. The information may be accurate, but it may be so voluminous that it is overwhelming and the purpose of having it is defeated.

There are also times when prior knowledge and information can interfere with our listening afresh and with an open mind. If a YMCA leader knows that a boy who has just joined the swimming group has a history of delinquency involving stealing, he may tend to listen to the boy a little differently than he would otherwise when the boy states his innocence with regard to missing towels. A teacher may be so anxious because of her knowledge that a particular student was once apprehended for hitting a teacher that she is unable to listen to him attentively and acceptingly when he comes up after class to ask her about an assignment. Our own reactions to the information we have, and how able we are to cope with it and not let it interfere with our listening with an open mind, will often be crucial in our efforts to be of help.

The helping art of listening, in summary, is an active searching for meaning in a highly involved participant-observer manner. Good listening requires not only careful attention to the literal and surface meaning of what is being said but also sensitive awareness to the contextual and subsurface meaning of what is being communicated. Although usually helpful listening will mean fostering the other person's capacity to express himself, occasionally it will require that we prevent him from inappropriate or hysterical verbalization. As with all our helping activities, good listening requires continual concern with the impact of our listening so that it will be truly helpful and not harmful.

9

The Art of Helping: Information Giving

►Every day we give information to someone about something. We do this so often and take the simplicity of the process so for granted that we are seldom aware of the many complexities actually involved. We usually give thought to the process of information giving only when we have been on the receiving end, when someone else has given us information, and we later find we really did not understand what was said or the information was inaccurate.

DIFFERENCE BETWEEN INFORMATION AND ADVICE

It is important that we clearly differentiate between the giving of information and the giving of advice. These two acts are often confused. It is a very common occurrence to ask for information and to receive advice; it is also common to feel we have informed someone when actually we have advised him. Whenever we find ourselves using such phrases as, "you should do this," or, "you ought to do that," then we are giving advice. The danger in giving advice is that we usually gloss over the responsibility of the other person for making his own decisions. When advice is sought and received from an expert, say a physician or a lawyer, usually the expert is careful to emphasize that "it is your decision." He essentially gives advice based on his awareness of information that we probably could not understand and usually could not judge as adequately as he with his greater training and education. But in giving such advice, based on his judgment of available information, he is careful to remind us that the responsibility for making a decision is ours.

In most situations where we are tempted to give advice, which will usually be either rejected too readily or accepted too passively, with a little extra work and thought we can present our thinking in an information giving approach that will be much sounder. The basic goal in giving information is to communicate the information in such a way that it will be understandable and usable by the person receiving it. We are concerned with helping the other person expand his knowledge and awareness so that responsible actions and decisions on his part will be more possible than if he were less well informed. The purpose is not so much persuading, as is the case with advice giving, but rather informing.

Let us look at two examples. Mrs. Green is planning a trip to Mexico and she is trying to obtain information about places to visit, hotel and restaurant facilities, roads, and so forth. She has two friends who have been to Mexico and she asks their help. As soon as she mentions her intention to travel to Mexico to her friend Sally, she is deluged with advice. With good helping intentions, Sally goes on at great length with such phrases as, "You don't want to take route X—that's an awful road. Take route Y instead. Be sure and stop at restaurant Z, you'll love it. And you don't want to miss the ruins in town M or the beach at L." Mrs. Green later contacts her friend Alice, who takes a somewhat different approach to her request. Alice, for example, tells her that route X is a winding mountain road that passes through many small villages, while route Y is a superhighway that bypasses most towns. She describes several restaurants and hotels along the way, and tells Mrs. Green that she could probably obtain many descriptive brochures by writing certain agencies. She comments on several of Mrs. Green's interests and suggests some specific places that would probably be of interest to her. Alice then goes on to describe some of her experiences and impressions, including her own preferences about some of the places mentioned.

Johnny is a high school senior and an average student. He is unsure of what to do after he graduates from high school. Three possibilities have occurred to him: he might go to college, he might join the Navy, or he might take a job. He has heard various individuals talk favorably about each of these alternatives, and he has also heard other people talk negatively about each of them. He is a member of several youth groups and decides to ask the group sponsors for information on the pros and cons of these alternative courses of action. The first sponsor he talks with is very definite and certain in his information and opinions. He quickly advises Johnny that he should, by all means, go on to college if if he can possibly arrange to do so. He stresses the value of education and points out that he can always join the Navy or take a job later on. The second sponsor responds in a different manner and spends considerable time talking with Johnny about his aspirations, goals, past experiences, and so on. After he has listened to Johnny for a while, he then gives him some factual information about each of the three alternatives. He carefully points out probable consequences that might follow each course of action, relating this to some of the information Johnny has already given about himself. Very clearly emphasizing that he is not Johnny, and that Johnny will have to make his own decision about what course of action to follow, he does state that if he were in the same situation he would probably try to go to college and would talk to the high school counselor about college possibilities.

These two examples serve to illustrate two different approaches in responding to someone's request for information. In each example the first person tended to take an advice giving approach while the second person tended to take an information giving approach. Several differences can be noted.

First, advice givers tend to confuse their own needs and preferences with those of the person they are trying to help. Their advice tends to reflect their own values and interests and to ignore the values and interests of those they are trying to help. Usually they do not even take the time to find out what is important to the person they are trying to help. In giving advice we too often act on the premise that what would be good for us would be good for the other person. In the foregoing examples, Alice and the second sponsor were both careful to differentiate between what was interesting and important to them and what might be interesting and important to the person they were trying to help. They presented information that helped the other person to obtain greater awareness and knowledge. The information presented by the advice givers, on the other hand, tended to be biased and distorted by their own views. If Mrs. Green, for example, preferred to travel on a winding road through villages so that she could get a better picture of the country and its people, then the remarks of Sally would have been of little help to her.

Second, advice givers do not differentiate between presenting objective information and presenting their own opinions. Information givers do not have to be impersonal, but they are careful to differentiate between the kinds of information they are presenting. The second sponsor, for example, let Johnny know what his preference would be but he was careful to do this in a way that did not confuse and bias the information he gave about the various alternatives.

Third, advice givers tend to present one course of action as best. Information givers tend to present various alternative courses of action and, insofar as possible, discuss various consequences that might follow from each alternative. They leave the person with choices, but give him information upon which to base his choices. They do not attempt to usurp the responsibility for making a decision that rightfully belongs to the person they are trying to help. They are also more likely than advice givers to furnish leads to additional information.

An information giving approach, in contrast to an advice giving approach, tends to foster long range, fundamental goals of helping others to help themselves. It fosters realistic functioning based on rational knowledge and leaves the person more confident of his capacity to make decisions. Sound advice is usually more readily accepted when we check our impulse to advise and, instead, present the relevant information so that the other person can reach his own conclusion.

WHAT IS ACTUALLY SOUGHT?

When someone else comes to us for information we must be alert as to what they are really asking for. Sometimes they are not asking for information as much as for advice. Here we must be careful that we do not foster their difficulty in making responsible decisions themselves. Rather than give advice, it is usually better to help them clarify their own thinking, organize their information, and make an attempt to reach a decision themselves. We can encourage their efforts in this direction, give them moral support and give them additional information if it is needed without "taking over" their responsibility for making their own decision.

We must also be sure that we understand what they are really saying and asking. We must get in step with them and not march to a tune of our own making. A brief story that is some years old illustrates this point very aptly. Seven-year-old Sally came running into the kitchen after school one day and asked her mother, "Mommy, where did I come from? How did I get here?" Mother took a deep breath, thought to herself that this was it, the moment she knew would be coming sooner or later, and suggested that Sally and she go to the living room where they could talk. About twenty minutes later, with mother feeling rather proud of her presentation of the essentials of the beginnings of life, Sally impatiently stated, "That's fine. But where did I come from? You know what I mean. Joe said he came from St. Louis by train and Betty said she came from Califronia by plane. Where did I come from?" If we are going to be helpful, we must first make sure we know what is being asked.

In giving information the temptation to impress others with our knowledge must be avoided. The purpose is to inform, not to impress. If we are unsure of the information ourselves, if we do not have accurate and up-to-date information, then we should feel comfortable in saying, "I don't know," and suggest the person ask someone else. Nothing is more aggravating and troublesome than to act on information that turns out to be wrong. Before we attempt to inform others, we should make sure we are well informed ourselves.

When we do have the relevant information that is being asked for, and we are sure that we understand what the person wants, then our next task is to present it to them in a manner that is understandable and useful to them. Our thoughts should be organized, our words clearly enunciated, and our terms meaningful to the person we are trying to help. When names and addresses are being given, we should be sure the person hears them correctly. In many situations it is most helpful if we write down directions, names, and addresses so that the person does not have to rely on his memory. These are relatively simple points, but day in and day out the neglect of them causes many people needless difficulty. Often they are overlooked because of our own great familiarity with what is being asked. We do not stop to realize that the person asking may be unfamiliar with people, places, and things that are everyday knowledge to us. For example, a person comes onto the grounds of a state institution, college campus, or large factory and asks how to find so-and-so. Frequently the reply will be, "He's in building X. It's a large brick building on the east side. You can't miss it." Because the person giving the information is so familiar with the grounds, he often does not sense how confusing they can be to a stranger—especially if the grounds are large, or there is no way to determine which way is east, or there is more than one brick building on the east side.

In many situations it is good procedure to have the person repeat to you the information you gave him. This gives you the opportunity to determine if he really understood you and it also helps him to remember the information longer. We often naïvely assume that the other person understands what we are saying when actually this is not the case. The other person may not want to expose his ignorance, he may not want to impose on us further, or he may be really frightened of us if we are in a position of authority or seniority in relation to him. In all these situations he may just nod and act as if he understands, when in reality he may not understand at all or he may have a distorted impression of what we said. Many people find it unbelievable that others might be somewhat frightened of them, or awed by them, but this occurs more often than is generally realized. Remember how the high school seniors looked when you were in sixth grade? And then how they looked after you had been out of high school several years? Others are sometimes awed by us because of our position, or age, or sex, and their own insecurity or inexperience at the time. Rather than take the chance of having the person leave with distorted information, it is usually better to make sure they have really understood us.

In some situations it is also helpful to present the information in two or even three different ways, using slightly different words and phrases. At times using an analogy from an area that is well-known to the person is also helpful. The important point, again, is that we communicate in a way the other person can understand what we are saying. Just because we understand ourselves is no assurance that the other person understands us.

WHAT MUST BE VOLUNTEERED?

Thus far we have discussed the situation in which someone comes to us for information. There is another kind of information giving situation that is frequently encountered wherein the initiative is reversed. Instead of someone coming to us, we go to them and initiate the giving of information ourselves. We often find ourselves in this latter situation when we are an employee or volunteer in an organization or agency. As an employee or volunteer we usually have two-way responsibilities, one to the person we are trying to help and another to the agency we represent. Agencies and organizations are not completely free entities; they have responsibilities and limitations formulated in regulations. There are times when our role as an employee or volunteer will require us to inform those we are attempting to help of our agency's policies and practices. There will be times when we must make decisions and take actions that are necessitated by the responsibilities and limitations of the organization we represent.

When we find that we must make decisions and initiate actions that will affect those we are trying to help, it is important that this be done with certainty and authority, but not in an authoritarian manner. It is often not enough to be right, correct, and accurate if we are seriously interested in helping others to help themselves. We must accept the other person's need and right to know why we have decided or acted as we did. We must share the reasoning behind our decisions and actions with those we are trying to help, and we must be ready to give meaningful explanations. This is often crucial if we are to have others "with us" and not "against us." One does not have to look far, unfortunately, in daily life to find many examples where sound decisions and actions were not accepted by others because the person initiating them had not taken the time or shown the consideration to explain the reasoning behind them.

A very dramatic example of the effect of giving or withholding explanations was presented in a television show several years ago. A group of settlers were heading westward in a wagon train under the leadership of a wagon master who, unfortunately, knew more about the technical aspects of his job than he did about people. Unforeseen events occurred as the wagon train moved westward, involving such things as Indian raids and accidents.

The wagon master, acting correctly on the basis of his more expert knowledge, found it necessary to impose certain restrictions, such as rationing of food and water, on the settlers. He also decided at one point to take a more difficult route across barren desert rather than follow the main trail. His decisions were right, but because he gave them in an authoritarian manner with no explanation, the settlers came to distrust him and they eventually rebelled, exiling him from the wagon train. Not having his expert technical knowledge, they made wrong decisions and later most of them died along the trail. A few years later another wagon train found itself in the same circumstances, and the wagon master made the same decisions. However, the second wagon master shared the reasons for his decisions with the settlers and, through explanation and discussion, was able to keep the settlers with him.

The foregoing example epitomizes a problem frequently encountered when we are attempting to help others, namely, the situation where certain decisions need to be made on the basis of more expert knowledge or on the basis of vested authority, but where their effectiveness depends on the acceptance of these decisions by those we are trying to help. To the extent possible, it is helpful and effective to involve those who will be affected by the decision in the decision-making process. This does not mean that they will always have an equal role in the decision-making process, but it does mean that they will have some part to play in it. They can be involved, for example, in an advisory capacity in discussion about the impending decision before it is actually made.

For example, a volunteer group is interested in providing companionship and stimulation to patients in a nursing home. Although the nursing home administrator will have final responsibility for deciding upon what services could be rendered and when, since he is responsible for the operation of the nursing home, it would still be wise and in keeping with a philosophy of helping others to help themselves to involve the patients in the decision-making process. Rather than the volunteers and administrator working out a plan for helping that seems good to them, it would be preferable to obtain the thinking of some of the patients about what would be helpful. This not only helps them to feel needed and useful, but it also frequently results in feasible ideas that did not occur to the volunteer or administrator. Because they are informed and involved through their own prior participation in the process, the patients are more likely to make use of and find acceptable whatever specific volunteer services are forthcoming.

NECESSITY TO INTERPRET LIMITS

All agencies and organizations have some rules and regulations that define responsibilities and limitations. These are not only necessary but they can also be helpful if implemented and interpreted with consideration for those affected by them. As a volunteer or employee, we often have to set limits with those we are trying to help. In some situations the limits will be defined by regulation, while in other situations the limits will be determined by us. For example, a youth sports program may offer swimming from four to seven and basketball from seven to nine. Hours of operation of the agency, as well as of specific programs and activities, are usually a matter of operating rules and regulations. A good youth leader, while acting with certainty and the authority vested in him, will go beyond merely informing the boys that the hours are such-and-such. He will explain the reasoning behind the regulations and obtain the boys' cooperation in abiding by the regulations through making sure the regulations are meaningful to them.

Rules and regulations that set limits are as necessary and can be as beneficial as other aspects of the helping relationship. They provide a degree of security and control, and if interpreted meaningfully they can serve to diminish conflict and disorganization. It is important, however, that limits be set in a non-punitive manner. When people are not adequately informed of the reasons for the limits, then there is the danger they will view them as punishments and fight against them.

Part of helping others involves helping them to function realistically and to be accepting that some rules and limits are needed in our complex world. Children and youth who learn to function comfortably within a framework of reasonable rules and regulations in their club and sport activities, who learn to use their capacities productively rather than expending energy continually fighting reasonable limits, will have taken a long step toward successful and comfortable adult functioning. This does not mean they will always passively accept whatever rules and regulations they find. It does mean they will work constructively to effect desired changes rather than lash out destructively and hurt themselves and others in the process. This means, also, that we must be especially alert to involve them, whenever possible, in a meaningful role in helping to set limits. The authoritarian presentation of limits, with no explanations or additional information, seldom helps others to see the limits as meaningful and worthy of their cooperation.

THE UNFAMILIAR

New situations tend to be anxiety-producing for many people. In the absence of any concrete information about what to expect, they will often imagine the worst and their fantasies will lead them to feel increasingly insecure and apprehensive. The early presentation of relevant information about what can be expected to happen can often prevent needless anxiety and suffering when people are confronted by unfamiliar situations.

The child entering the hospital for the first time, the boy going on his first overnight camping trip, the young miss going to her first ball, and the executive facing his first board meeting are all usually somewhat anxious and apprehensive as to what will take place. They have probably heard others talk about such events, usually with an exaggerated emphasis on the things that can go wrong. Rumors and gossip thrive on the negative rather than the positive, with the result that we are all too often well primed with false or distorted information about events and situations that we have yet to experience ourselves.

Although having specific, sound information about what will probably take place will not prevent all anxiety, such information can often go a long way toward lessening the discomfort experienced. It may make the difference between the individual being able to cope with his anxieties in a manner that allows him to function adequately and his being overwhelmed by his anxieties to the point where he is unable to function appropriately. The information presented before the event need not be elaborate to be helpful. For example, if the child entering the hospital has some knowledge that he will see women in white uniforms and smell odors that are strange, or if the executive has some knowledge of the physical structure and preferred seating arrangements in the board room, then these individuals will feel less strange and ill at ease in the new situation.

When we have accurate information about what will probably

take place, then we can prepare ourselves accordingly. Part of the preparation for any new experience involves a kind of rehearsal wherein we mentally anticipate and accustom ourselves to what will probably take place. In this way the unfamiliar becomes less strange to us. When we find ourselves in the situation and things proceed as we had anticipated, based upon our prior knowledge, then we feel reassured and more comfortable.

It is important that misleading information not be given to individuals about what will probably happen in an attempt to provide them with a temporary sense of security. When we do this we are usually trying to make things easier for ourselves rather than the person we are trying to help. For example, the mother who persuades Junior to go to the dentist peacefully under the illusion that the dentist is only going to look in his mouth, when in actuality mother knows that the dentist is going to have to remove a tooth, is really doing her child no favor. Not only will Junior probably become more panic-stricken when the dentist proceeds with his work, but he will also become more distrustful of his mother. False assurances are almost never helpful in the long run; on the contrary, they usually contribute to eventual increased confusion, mistrust, and discomfort.

"UNWELCOME" INFORMATION

Although in many situations the information we give is gladly welcomed, there are some situations in which the information can be expected to give rise to at least temporary discomfort and anxiety. A dormitory counselor, for example, has noticed that one of the girls in the dorm is consistently avoided by the other girls. This particular girl has few friends and no dates despite her pleasant mannerisms and her attempts to seek friends. It is no secret to anyone except her that matters of personal hygiene and cleanliness are causing at least some of her difficulties. As the ads say, "even her best friend won't tell her." The dormitory counselor senses the girl's despair and wants to help her, yet she feels embarrassed and uneasy at the prospect of taking the initiative and talking with the girl.

In such situations, of course, we are confronted primarily with our own discomfort and embarrassment at the prospect of being the initiator of what will be experienced, at least temporarily, as unpleasant news. Usually we will find also that we are somewhat fearful of being rejected and disliked by the other person for not minding our own business. Again, helping others is not always easy or popular or comfortable. It would certainly be easier and more comfortable for the counselor to do nothing—if she could live with this choice. If she is really concerned, however, and really wants to be of help, then she cannot avoid what she anticipates will be an unpleasant task.

If we are really serious about wanting to help others, then we must be prepared to be the conveyor of what appears to be bad news at times, and we must be more concerned with helping than with our own popularity. In situations similar to that of the dormitory counselor, the task is clear. In a sincere, humble, direct, and brief manner we can present the unpleasant information and tolerate the hostility or tears that may result. We should say what we have to say briefly, allow the person to react with emotion, and then help them through further discussion to find a way of solving the problem. More often than not we will find, a few days or weeks later, that the person will communicate his thanks to us when he could not do so at the time. Also, once having coped with our own feelings in such situations, we will find that our anticipated fantasies of what might happen were exaggerated, indeed, on the negative side.

It is not very helpful to confine our comments about the shortcomings of others to coffee-table talk in their absence. Even though we may be verbally expressing concern about the other person, on another and more meaningful level we are really showing our lack of concern. If we really do care, then we will talk directly with the person in private and avoid discussing his shortcomings in public.

REFERRALS

In our helping relationships with others we will frequently become aware of another's need for specialized help beyond that which we are qualified to give. We will find it necessary, at times, to suggest that the individual seek more qualified help. When behavioral and emotional problems are involved, this presents a difficulty to some people because they have not worked through their own feelings about what it means to seek help in this area. Responsible helping behavior requires, however, that we do become comfortable with referring others to specialized sources of help when the need arises. We must, if we are to be effective helpers, become comfortable in discussing with others their need for the specialized help that can be obtained from psychologists, psychiatrists, and other highly trained mental health specialists.

A first step in becoming comfortable in making good referrals is to become familiar and knowledgeable about specialized resources and what they have to offer. Consultation with a mental health specialist about making referrals can be helpful. A visit to the office of such a specialist can be helpful. Certainly it will be difficult to suggest to a person that they might benefit from the services of a psychologist if we ourselves are unclear about what a psychologist is or does. Once we become knowledgeable about specialized resources in our area and informed of the kinds of services they offer, then we will find it much easier to discuss the use of these services with those we are trying to help.

The art of giving information in a helpful manner requires that we first become informed and knowledgeable ourselves. We then must be able to comunicate our information in an understandable and comfortable manner to others. We must know what we want to say and how to say it. Simple though this may sound, the clear presentation of misinformation and the confused presentation of accurate information remain a common source of many difficulties.

10
Beyond The Helping Relationship

▶In this book we have been primarily concerned with the art of establishing effective helping relationships for the purpose of helping others to help themselves. Our goal has been the fostering of mature and responsible behavior that enables individuals to lead productive and personally satisfying lives. Specifically, we have been concerned with using ourselves in relation to others in a way that fosters their becoming more realistic, self-confident, self-directing, self-actualizing, rejoiceful of life, and considerate toward others.

Although it is not the purpose of this book to explore in detail the vast amount of effort and work that goes on beyond the helping relationship to create a more helpful and helping society, it would be a gross oversight not to mention at least briefly some of these activities. A wide variety of activities are necessary to sustain the direct helping relationships found in our helping organizations and agencies. Just as the soldier on the firing line is supported and exists only by virtue of the many individuals functioning behind the battlefield, so also the helping person working directly with individuals and groups can function only because of the efforts of many others who never come in direct contact with those needing and receiving help. These individuals, no less than the person giving help directly, are essential to the task of creating a helping society oriented toward helping others to help themselves.

AGENCY POLICIES AND PRACTICES

A helping agency or organization usually comes into being to meet certain unmet needs. The policies and practices of the agency should reflect, insofar as possible, the general philosophy and purpose of the agency. Efficiency in various aspects of the agency's operations should not undermine effectiveness in carrying out its primary goals. For example, a punitive billing and collection procedure where fees are involved or a high-pressure fund raising campaign using ethically questionable practices would not be in keeping with a helping organization's primary philosophy and system of values. Efficiency in agency operations is important, but it must be judged and evaluated in terms of the agency's overall goals and not just in terms of one part of the agency's functioning.

The effectiveness of governing board members in setting policy and the effectiveness of administrators in translating policy into practice will be crucial to the success of the agency and to the effectiveness of helping people who are working directly with individuals served by the agency. Governing policies and operating procedures must consistently and harmoniously foster the atmosphere and program mechanisms whereby helping activities can be conducted and helping relationships can be created. When persons directly responsible for creating helping relationships with individuals seeking help are confused or in conflict about agency policies and practices, then effectiveness will be impaired and those seeking help will be the real losers.

Money is the lifeblood for most organizations and agencies. Adequate finances must be available if needed services and programs are to be offered. Money is the medium which enables us to translate many values into practice. The importance of participation in fund raising activities cannot be overemphasized. Both as givers and as helpers in fund raising activities, we are participants in creating and sustaining helping programs and services. When participating in fund raising activities, it is important to remember that we are viewed by those we contact as representatives of the helping organization. For some people we will be the sole agency representative they will ever meet, and they will form an impression of the agency from the way we relate to them and discuss the agency and its programs with them. At the very least, we should be knowledgeable about the agency and able to discuss its programs in a positive way.

INITIAL AWARENESS OF THE AGENCY

There is a saying among mental health specialists that treatment begins when the patient first enters the office. This is only partially true because it does not go far enough. In helping organizations and agencies the helping process begins even before this. It begins when the person who might later seek help first becomes aware of the existence of the organization or agency. This may occur by seeing a brochure, by hearing a speaker, or by word of mouth from a friend. At this initial point of awareness of the existence of a helping resource the person begins to form an impression of the resource as it potentially may affect him. This initial impression may be very vague, but usually there is a "leaning toward" or a "leaning away" reaction by the person. That is, he develops a feeling of acceptance or rejection toward the helping resource from this initial awareness.

Helping agencies and organizations must be available before people can make use of them. Once they are available, however, they must become known to potential users in a way that leaves the potential users with the feeling that these are places where they can go to receive help. Public information, public education, and public relations programs are important activities in any helping organization or agency. When they are conducted effectively, they are instrumental in helping to prepare people to make effective use of the services offered by the organization or agency.

A person's first actual contact with a helping organization or agency is another crucial point in the helping process. Often the first representative of the agency he will talk to will be the receptionist, secretary, or switchboard operator. Although they sometimes do not view themselves in this way, these people are, in fact, representatives of the agency. Their attitudes, effectiveness, courtesy, and capacity to relate to people will often be important determiners of how the agency is perceived by individuals in the community. How they answer questions and schedule appointments will often determine whether an individual will want to make use of the services offered.

Business and office staff also will be important determiners of the agency's success in being a helping resource. Inaccurate or misfiled records, wrongly recorded telephone numbers and addresses, misspelled names, and so on, can create an impression of confusion and inefficiency which will carry over into other aspects of the agency's functioning. Business and office personnel should be well informed about the agency's services, imbued with its helping philosophy, and act as positive supporters of its programs.

In connection with specific helping organizations and agencies, then, we find that a number of roles and activities are necessary if the helping person directly in contact with individuals in need of help is to be effective. We may also find, from time to time, that we are participants in different phases of the overall helping endeavor. A woman may be a paid secretary in a helping organization in the morning, a Den Mother working directly with children in the afternoon, and a participant in a fund raising drive in the evening. On another evening she may be a member of an advisory committee or a governing board of a helping agency. In all these roles her view of herself as a vital participant in a helping process is highly important to her effectiveness.

COMMUNITY PROGRAMS

There are also many activities which may or may not be associated with specific agencies that are highly influential in helping others to help themselves. Coordinated planning to provide for the orderly development of comprehensive helping services is an increasing necessity in our complex society. Haphazard development of helping services without prior long-range planning usually results in an overabundance of services to some people and a lack of services to others. Prior rational planning that takes into account such factors as the overall needs of the people, the availability and allocation of finances and skilled manpower, and the interrelation of helping services makes possible more adequate services for a greater number of people.

The development of sound community programs and resources takes time and persistent effort. From the time a few individuals first decide to do something about a specific community need to the time that the resource is actually functioning, usually many meetings have been held and the time can be counted in years. Soundly developed programs that make a lasting contribution involve vast amounts of time, energy, effort, and work. Programs quickly established with little community support and involvement often fade as quickly. Even worse, they may sometimes impede more lasting developments that were maturing more slowly. Quickly established, stopgap programs have a way of creating the illusion that the need has been met, whereas actually only a part of it may have been met or it may have been met in a way that is "second-best." The concern in planning activities is as much for those yet unborn as it is for those currently in need of help.

Participation on survey teams, fact-finding committees, study groups, planning councils, and advisory boards can be as effective a way of helping others to help themselves as participation in direct helping relationships. A person may be very cold, aloof and critical of others with little capacity to talk directly with individuals in a helping manner, yet he may be more effective than most in evaluating existing programs and making sound recommendations for change. Sound recommendations for change based upon evaluation of the effectiveness of existing services can lead to new programs and services resulting in better service to more people. Evaluation of existing services and planning for new services to meet future needs should be on-going, continual processes whereever helping services are provided.

LEGISLATION AND RESEARCH

Another sphere of activity with great potential for helping others to help themselves is the legislative process. Concern and involvement with impending legislation are imperative if we are really interested in helping others to help themselves. Our Constitution and Bill of Rights, as well as much significant legislation through the years, have established the basic ground rules for a society in which equal opportunity for growth and development is a fundamental objective. The review of existing legislation and the promotion of revisions and new legislation where necessary for the purposes of fostering the kind of society that enables individuals to maximize their potentials is the obligation of all citizens interested in helping others to help themselves. Only through continual involvement by enlightened citizens in legislative processes at state and national levels can we maintain the progress we have made and continue toward the goal of "life, liberty, and happiness" for everyone.

Perhaps further removed from the everyday awareness of most citizens, yet of fundamental importance to all helping activities at all levels, is the work of the researcher in producing and refining knowledge. Sound agency practice, sound planning, and sound legislative proposals are ultimately dependent upon sound basic knowledge. Research findings in a wide variety of areas are having increasing implications for helping activities. More effective preventive programs in the future as well as more effective direct services for people with problems will be a consequence of the work of many researchers today. Future progress, far more than past progress, in providing effective helping services will depend on insights and breakthroughs obtained from basic research.

A distinction is sometimes made between basic research and applied research. There is a common misconception that applied research has practical value whereas basic research has no practical value. Actually basic research has immense practical value, but the payoff in terms of application to practical problems is usually delayed and long-range rather than immediate as is usually the case with applied research. Achievements at a basic research level, wherein no *immediate* practical application of results may be apparent, are often more significant for *eventual* solutions of practical problems than are achievements at an applied research level. We now know that much of the success of applied research, which is usually directly related to a practical problem confronting us, depends upon the state of knowledge at a more basic level. Basic research on problems of no apparent immediate practical importance must be supported and conducted if really significant breakthroughs on a practical level are to be achieved at later dates. The research team studying the behavior of monkeys in a laboratory or the research team investigating the uses of computers in playing chess may well have a significant impact on helping others to help themselves over the long-range span of time.

Helping others to help themselves is no small undertaking. It requires our efforts at many different levels and in a wide variety of activities. Not only are we all involved to some extent in direct helping activities, but we are also needed in those activities beyond the helping relationship that are influential in helping others to become more realistic, self-confident, self-directing, self-actualizing, rejoiceful of life, and considerate of others. The opportunities exist and the responsibility cannot be denied for relating to others in a helping manner. Like it or not, we are involved. Our only choices are with respect to the extent and the effectiveness of our involvement.

"[This book] offers an extremely useful tool to all of us who are involved in attempting to improve the quality of human existence in our time. It is a reaffirmation of our conviction that human beings can and must be of help to each other, and that it is only through such interdependency and mutual assistance that society can serve the needs of its individual members.

"Dr. Mahoney has brought to this book a sophisticated and mature understanding of the key contributions of the several behavioral sciences, and has translated them into pragmatic and workable suggestions for professional and nonprofessional, full and part-time helper alike.

"Whether the reader is a neighborhood aide in the War on Poverty, a psychiatric technician in a hospital or clinic, a volunteer working in a health or social agency, a case aide beginning service in a welfare department, a school or college counselor —he will find this book of inestimable assistance in increasing his effectiveness in helping others." — H. G. WHITTINGTON, M.D., Director, Division of Psychiatric Services, Denver (Col.) General Hospital.